WE TALK,
YOU LISTEN

WE TALK, YOU LISTEN

New Tribes, New Turf

BY VINE DELORIA, JR.

A DELTA BOOK

A DELTA BOOK

Published by
Dell Publishing Co., Inc.
750 Third Avenue
New York, New York 10017

Delta ® TM 755118, Dell Publishing Co., Inc.
Reprinted by arrangement with The Macmillan Company.
Printed in the United States of America
First Delta printing—March 1972

CONTENTS

INTRODUCTION

Every now and then I am impressed with the thinking of the non-Indian. I was in Cleveland last year and got to talking with a non-Indian about American history. He said that he was really sorry about what had happened to Indians, but that there was good reason for it. The continent had to be developed and he felt that Indians had stood in the way and thus had had to be removed. "After all," he remarked, "what did you do with the land when you had it?" I didn't understand him until later when I discovered that the Cuyahoga River running through Cleveland is inflammable. So many combustible pollutants are dumped into the river that the inhabitants have to take special precautions during the summer to avoid accidentally setting it on fire. After reviewing the argument of my non-Indian friend I decided that he was probably correct. Whites had made better use of the land. How many Indians could have thought of creating an inflammable river?

A century ago whites broke the Fort Laramie Treaty with the Sioux so they could march into the Black Hills and dig gold out of the ground. Then they took the gold out of the Black Hills, carried it to Fort Knox, Kentucky, and buried it in the ground. Throughout the Midwest, Indians were forced off their lands because whites felt that the Indians didn't put the lands to good use. Today most of this land lies idle every year while the owners collect a government check for not planting anything. Wilderness was taken because "no one" lived there and cities were built in which no one could live.

These little insights into the workings of non-Indian society give me pause on my daily journeys. Whenever I become depressed I always turn to the younger generation and New Left groups for solace. Instinctively, they seem to understand Indians, and one can find cheer in their wisdom. In describing his beloved Woodstock Nation at the Chicago Conspiracy trial, Abbie Hoffman, the Diogenes of our time, said that it was located in the state of *mind.* "It's a nation of alienated young people which we carry around in our minds just as the Sioux Indians carried around the Sioux Nation in their minds," Hoffman said.

Abbie's chances of relating to the Sioux are comparable to Custer's. Although we did not torture prisoners as a rule, traditions have been waived for special occasions and Hoffman's visit to a Sioux reservation would certainly be considered an important occasion. Abbie should have been at a certain civil rights hearing a few years back. One of the whites asked J. Dan Howard, a Standing Rock Sioux tribal councilman, if the Sioux still considered themselves a nation. "You bet," was Dan's reply, "we could still declare war on you. You *might* beat us but we'd take a lot of you with us."

Again, last summer, a noted female anthropologist presented a scholarly paper to the effect that Indians drink to gain an identity. Anyone who has ever seen Indians would laugh at the absurdity of this idea. It is unquestionably the other way. Indians first ask what your name is, then what your tribe is. After these preliminaries you are sometimes asked to have a drink. Drinking is only the confirmation of a friendship already established by the fact that you belong to a specific tribe. If we acted the way anthropologists describe us, we would get lousy stinking drunk, THEN DECIDE WHAT TRIBE WE WANTED TO BELONG TO, and finally choose a surname for ourselves.

All of these things have set me wondering if there isn't a better way to distinguish between the Indian mood, life style, and philosophy, and that of the non-Indian. It is very difficult to do. Non-Indians are descended from a peculiar group of people. The first group thought they were sailing off the edge of the world and probably would have had we not pulled them ashore. Their successors spent years traveling all over the continent in search of the Fountain of Youth and the Seven Cities of Gold. They didn't even know how to plant an ear of corn when they arrived on these shores. So the non-Indian is pretty set in his ideas and hard to change.

There are a great many things happening today that can be related to ideas, movements, and events in Indian country—so many that it is staggering to contemplate them. American society is unconsciously going Indian. Moods, attitudes, and values are changing. People are becoming more aware of their isolation even while they continue to worship the rugged individualist who needs no one. The self-sufficient man is casting about for a community to call his own. The glittering generalities and mythologies of American society no longer satisfy the need and desire to belong.

Trying to communicate is an insurmountable task, however, since one cannot skip readily from a tribal way of life to the conceptual world of the non-tribal person. The non-tribal person thinks in a linear sequence, in which A is the foundation for B, and C always follows. The view and meaning of the total event is rarely understood by the non-tribal person, although he may receive more objective information concerning any specific element of the situation. Non-tribals can measure the distance to the moon with unerring accuracy, but the moon remains an impersonal object to them without personal relationships that would support or illuminate their innermost feelings.

Tribal society is of such a nature that one must experience it from the inside. It is holistic, and logical analysis will only return you to your starting premise none the wiser for the trip. Being inside a tribal universe is so comfortable and reasonable that it acts like a narcotic. When you are forced outside the tribal context you become alienated, irritable, and lonely. In desperation you long to return to the tribe if only to preserve your sanity. While a majority of Indian people today live in the cities, a substantial number make long weekend trips back to their reservations to spend precious hours in their own land with their people.

The best method of communicating Indian values is to find points at which issues appear to be related. Because tribal society is integrated toward a center and non-Indian society is oriented toward linear development, the process might be compared to describing a circle surrounded with tangent lines. The points at which the lines touch the circumference of the circle are the issues and ideas that can be shared by Indians and other groups. There are a great many points at which tangents occur, and they may be considered as windows through which Indians and non-Indians can glimpse each other. Once this structural device is used and understood, non-Indians, using a tribal point of view, can better understand themselves and their relationship to Indian people.

The problem is complicated by the speed of modern communications media. It floods us with news that is news because it is reported as news. Thus, if we take a linear viewpoint of the world, the sequence of spectacular events creates the impression that the world is going either up- or downhill. Events become noted more for their supportive or threatening aspects than for their reality, since they fall into line and do not themselves contain any means of interpretation. When we are unable to absorb the events reported to us by the media, we begin to force interpretations of what the world really means on the basis of what we have been taught rather than what we have experienced.

Indian people are just as subject to the deluge of information as are other people. In the last decade most reservations have come within the reach of television and computers. In many ways Indian people are just as directed by the electric nature of our universe as any other group. But the tribal viewpoint simply absorbs what is reported to it and immediately integrates it into the experience of the group. In many areas whites are regarded as a temporary aspect of tribal life and there is unshakable belief that the tribe will survive the domination of the white man and once again rule the continent. Indians soak up the world like a blotter and continue almost untouched by events. The more that happens, the better the tribe seems to function and the stronger it appears to get. Of all the groups in the modern world Indians are best able to cope with the modern situation. To the non-Indian world, it does not appear that Indians are capable of anything. The flexibility of the tribal viewpoint enables Indians to meet devastating situations and survive. But this flexibility is seen by non-Indians as incompetency, so that as the non-Indian struggles in solitude and despair he curses the Indian for not coveting the same disaster.

In 1969, non-Indians began to rediscover Indians. Everyone hailed us as their natural allies in the ancient struggle they were waging with the "bad guys." Conservatives embraced us because we didn't act uppity, refused to move into their neighborhoods, and didn't march in *their* streets. Liberals loved us because we were the most oppressed of all the peoples who had been oppressed, and besides we generally voted Democratic.

Blacks loved us because we objected to the policies of the Department of the Interior (we would probably object if we had set the damn thing up ourselves) which indicated to them that we were another group to count on for the coming revolution. I attended one conference last fall at which a number of raging militants held forth, giving their views on the upcoming revolt of the masses. In a fever pitch they described the battle of Armageddon in which the "pigs" would be vanquished and the meek would inherit the earth (or a reasonable facsimile thereof). When asked if he supported the overthrow of the establishment, an old Sioux replied, "not until we get paid for the Black Hills." Needless to say, revolutionaries have not been impressed with the Indian fervor for radical change.

Hippies proudly showed us their beads and, with a knowing smile, bid us hello in the Navajo they had learned while passing through Arizona the previous summer. We watched and wondered as they paraded by in buckskin and feathers, anxiously playing a role they could not comprehend. When the Indians of the Bay area occupied Alcatraz, the hippies descended on the island in droves, nervously scanning the horizon for a vision of man in his pristine natural state. When they found that the tribesmen had the same organizational problems as any other group might have, they left in disappointment, disillusioned with "Indianism" that had existed only in their imaginations.

For nearly a year, the various minority and power groups have tried to get Indians to relate to the social crisis that plagues the land. Churches have expended enormous sums creating "task forces" of hand-picked Indians to inform them on the national scope of Indian problems. They have been disappointed when Indians didn't immediately embrace violence as a technique for progress. Government agencies have tried to understand Indians in an urban context that no longer has validity for even the most stalwart urbanite. Conservationists have sought out Indians for their mystical knowledge of the use of land. It has been an exciting year.

There is no doubt in my mind that a major crisis exists. I believe, however, that it is deeper and more profound than racism, violence, and economic deprivation. American society is undergoing a total replacement of its philosophical concepts. Words are being emptied of old meanings and new values are coming in to fill the vacuum. Racial antagonisms, inflation, ecological destruction, and power groups are all symptoms of the emergence of a new world view of man and his society. Today thought patterns are shifting from the traditional emphasis on the solitary individual to as yet unrelated definitions of man as a member of a specific group.

This is an extremely difficult transition for any society to make. Rather than face the situation head-on, people have preferred to consider social problems as manifestations of a gap between certain elements of the national community. The most blatant example of this attitude is to speak of the "generation gap." Other times it is categorized as a racial problem—the white racist power structure against the pure and peace-loving minority groups. We know that this is false. In those programs where blacks have dominated they have been as racist against Indians as they claim whites have been against them. Behind every movement is the undeniable emergence of the group as a group. Until conceptions of the nature of mass society are enlarged and accepted by the majority of people there will be little peace in this society.

But one cannot go skipping from group to group checking out movements and ideas to see if everything will come out all right. A better way of understanding events would be to find the similarities of structure that exist. Generalizations on this basis, if the necessary philosophical distinctions are maintained, would be most helpful. It would appear to me that modern society has two alternatives at this point. American people are being pushed into new social forms because of the complex nature of modern communications and transportation, and the competing forms are neotribalism and neofeudalism. The contest of the future is between a return to the castle or the tipi.

The difference between the castle and the tipi is immense, yet there are such great similarities that it is difficult to distinguish between them. Each offers social identity and economic security within a definite communal system. But the leveling process of the tribal form prevents the hereditary control over a social pyramid, and the feudalistic form has the efficiency to create and control technology. Both are needed if we are to rule machines instead of submit to them.

Many people can and will support the return of the castle. We have already experienced Camelot and the universal longing for its return. The massive corporate organizations have driven us well into the era of neofeudalism. But the continual failure of the total economic system to support the population and the corporations speaks of the necessity to reorient social goals more in line with a tribal-communal life style. Tribalism can only be presented in mosaic form. And there is a certain novelty in this approach. No single idea inevitably leads to another. The total impact of tribalism is thus not dependent upon acceptance of a single thesis. If events and ideas do not strike one immediately, time does not erode them but serves to shed further light on the problem.

After viewing social problems from a number of angles, I can see but one conclusion: America needs a new religion. Nearly every event and movement today shows signs of fulfilling this role, but none has the centered approach that would permit it to dig its roots in and survive. I am not advocating a return to Christianity. That "religion" has had two thousand years of bloodshed and hypocrisy and has failed to do anything more than help turn men into machines. We are probably entering an era in which religious sensitivity is expressed in rigorous adherence to the values of racial and ethnic groups—secularization of religious feelings in political action.

If my conclusion is correct, then it is necessary to outline the Indian point of view as a contribution to the discussion of the problem. Further generalizations about how we are all alike—all people—are useless today. Definite points of view, new logic, and different goals define us. All we can do is try to communicate what we feel our group means to itself and how we relate to other groups. Understanding each other as distinct peoples is the most important thing.

As to the point of view, there really is a difference. A man was explaining his war experiences to his son one day. "There we were, surrounded by thousands of the enemy. Bullets were whizzing around our heads. Our water was gone. We had no food and our ammunition was running out. Suddenly, in the distance, we heard the welcome sound—of war whoops."

1 * THE COMMUNICATIONS GAP

THE GAP WE HAVE between the generations and between white society and the minority groups stems directly from a failure to understand that for all of us the world has changed irretrievably. Because of the instantaneousness of modern communications, the medium through which we receive our experiences has become the message we receive. Until we can reflect on the meaning of this change we will continue to struggle without understanding why we are struggling and what we hope to solve by doing so.

The revolutionary nature of our world can scarcely be conceived. Western civilization has always depended upon the ability to symbolize, categorize, specialize, and divide according to function. In this manner science, supported by the thesis of the theists that the world is rational, has prospered. Western man has systematically divided his knowledge of the world into disciplines having academic status. All new experience has been differentiated into the major categories and the respective fields of knowledge have been related to individuals through the educational process.

But the various fields of knowledge have rarely been related to each other. They had to be mutually exclusive so that each field could have a validity of its own. Without a unity of knowledge it has been impossible to reconcile the respective fields of knowledge so that the totality of issues can be seen. Thus the world of the politician has been infinitely different than that of the academician or the businessman. The elements of society have been placed at cross-purposes because their orientation toward issues has differed radically. Thus we have seen the spectacle of anthropologist Margaret Mead, speaking from a lifetime of experience in observing the social mechanics of societies, being called a "dirty old lady" by the Governor of Florida because their viewpoints on the issue of marijuana have arisen from entirely different premises.

The effect on society of this method of comprehending the world has been such that decisions in the political and social fields have come to be based upon the exercise of naked power by those in a position to define policies. While there can be equally valid interpretations of problems by sociologists, economists, historians, political scientists, and religious leaders, the solution to problems has been a simple compromise between the two explanations best able to muster political strength to support themselves.

Politically there has been a polarization between conservative and liberal understandings of the world revolving around the role of the federal government. With the corollaries of massive spending versus a balanced budget determining the practical aspects of the federal role, a generation has been devoted to developing a compromise regarding the nature of the federal government in American life.

The struggle really began with the advent of radio, although few people understood at the time what was happening. Radio reprocessed the mechanized environment of early twentieth-century industrial society to an amazing degree. The older generation of today, children during the Depression, observed their immigrant parents working hard to provide a living and education for them. This kind of life was the *means*, the *medium* by which their parents adjusted to the life style of a frontier America.

This medium became the message, and the criteria of values and the virtues of hard work were voiced abroad as the principles of true Americanism. But the Depression belied the gospel of hard work because it presented an irrational aspect to the smooth functioning of the free enterprise system. So the Depression generation created a new medium for themselves. Fearing desperate economic conditions, radio brought them the message from Franklin Roosevelt's fireside that all they had to fear was fear itself. Roosevelt and the New Deal would take care of everything else.

Instead of living the credo of their parents, the stolid individualism of the past, the Depression generation voted themselves every conceivable benefit which a government could bestow. The Federal Housing Authority, the Federal Deposit Insurance Corporation, the Agricultural Adjustment Act, the Social Security system and many other programs were all products of the Depression generation. From cradle to grave they gave themselves benefits and never stopped talking about how they had "made it" on their own.

Government programs and federal solutions to local problems were the media of the Depression generation. When the Second World War came, they promptly invented cost plus contracts, the G.I. Bill of Rights, and massive defense contracts that have now become the most important part of the American economy. These programs produced such a prosperity that it was necessary to extend the war economy over the last two decades to prevent wholesale collapse of the social structure.

These media used by the Depression generation have now become the issue, the substance of inquiry for the present generation. The reinterpretation of the Interstate Commerce Clause to provide the necessities of life in the Depression has provided a basis for inquiry into the nature of American society. Young people today have refused to believe that life revolves around man as an economic animal. They have taken the media of the Depression generation, the role of a government to provide prosperous conditions to its constituency, as the issue for themselves. Thus there is constant probing into the fabric of American society and government to discover what the good life is.

Marshall McLuhan describes this process as the coalescing of the medium and the message into one experienced event over which we have no control. He means that "in terms of the electronic age a totally new environment has been created. The 'content' of this new environment is the old mechanized environment of the industrial age. The new environment reprocesses the old one as radically as TV is reprocessing the film."

It is not even as simple as that. Symbolism has taken a turn toward the undefinable, because the language structure, insofar as it communicates meanings, has collapsed as the old environment has been reprocessed. If the medium is the message then there really is no symbolism. External definition of image and symbol as objects of knowledge is no longer possible. Internal and external are now one.

The resultant confusion in American society has been incredible. Burning the American flag has become both patriotic and unpatriotic. Society has been polarized around the meanings of its symbolic events, not realizing that symbolic events are impossible. Conservatives fear that unless we *win* in Vietnam we will be destroyed as a nation. Liberals feel that if we do win it will mean the end of us as a nation because we will be committed to destroying the world to stop imagined threats to our national ego.

Behind the ideologies of both extremes one logical method of analysis stands out—Western man, particularly American Western man, is committed to an either/or logic when neither alternative is real. The very tools of thinking and expressing ourselves have been negated by the means we use to think and express ourselves. We continue to deal with a two-dimensional moral universe of right and wrong when the morality of the data we receive is defined by our ability to receive the data.

What passes for thinking today is the old process of relating the unknown and unexpected to familiar categories of explanation which have been arranged on a symbolic basis by our educational experience. If an event does not relate to the categories we have committed to memory early in our youth, then it has no ultimate existence for us or it is forced into those categories and forgotten. Society is trapped between a world which it experiences and a world it has been taught to recognize. Never have so many foolish statements been sent abroad in search of true believers.

McLuhan says that the normal action of our technology is "submerging the natives with floods of concepts for which nothing has prepared them." It is this factor more than any other that has allowed Western technology to overcome the cultures of the underdeveloped countries. But now, with the electric media, Western man himself is innundated. "We are no more prepared to encounter radio and TV in our literate milieu," McLuhan notes, "than the native of Ghana is able to cope with the literacy that takes him out of his collective tribal world and beaches him in individual isolation. We are as numb in our new electric world as the native involved in our literate and mechanical culture."

The result of concept-inundation is that traditional mythology used to explain the world has collapsed along with the symbolism that made up the mythology. We have seen the mythology of America as a just, peace-loving society rudely torn apart by the report of the National Commission on the Causes and Prevention of Violence and the continual emphasis on the rise of violent crime in the United States. According to the report we have been lulled into a "historical amnesia that masks much of [our] turbulent past. Probably all nations share this tendency to sweeten their memories of their past through collective repression, but Americans have probably magnified this process of selective recollection, owing to our historic vision of ourselves as a latter-day chosen people, a New Jerusalem."

This mythology—the chosen people, manifest destiny—has broken down completely for many of us. In its place the ugly revelation of Songmy stands as mute testimony to a world of reality that intrudes on our sensibilities and fantasies. We are unable to distinguish between what is happening and what it means. We tend to credit the difference in reception that exists in ourselves to outside and malevolent influences. We are inundated with data and concepts from one medium and we receive them in a knowledge structure forged by another medium. At the Chicago Democratic Convention in 1968, the cameras were *reporting* the street disturbances from the limited viewpoint of a stationary observation point allowed to the press. But people blamed television for *emphasizing* violence. Few people could understand that what they were viewing on their screen was not a contrived form of entertainment but was actually happening.

Another aspect of fading mythology that plagues us today is our assumption that all things are relative and that one man's judgment is as good as another's. American society has always been tolerant of divergent views within its white mainstream. This liberalism was twisted completely out of shape when it was unexpectedly buttressed by Einstein's Theory of Relativity, enunciated early in the century. Popularization of this theory made it appear that no ultimate criteria existed, and the great expansion of viewpoints we have had in this century is based upon a lack of acceptable standards for making judgments.

In policies and programs we have tended to favor one thing over another because neither had any aspect of ultimate reality. We balance the Everglades against a jetport and the jetport wins because it has an immediate economic value that can be reduced to a figure in the gross national product. We balance San Francisco Bay against the need for additional land, and the business community wins, all things being relative.

We have not understood that a change in one element of a situation invariably creates a change in all others. Few have realized that we can no longer stand as impartial and rational observers of events, because in merely observing those events we become participants in them. More than that, we are intimate segments of the events themselves whether we choose to be or not. Nothing is really relative, everything is related. The spectacle of a dead Lake Erie, the other Great Lakes dying, a flammable Cayuhoga River in Cleveland, the oil-drenched beaches of California, and the ultimate destruction of the oxygen in our atmosphere bear mute testimony that all things are related.

Although American society has accepted the relativity of things as a leveling device between comparative values, white society has, on the whole, acted as if all things should be related to its values only. An excellent example of this attitude is the reception given the Mexican Americans when they appealed for foundation help. For nearly a decade foundations have responded to the pleas of the black community and had given grants for every conceivable black project. During that time, grants to Indians and Mexicans were considered to be some kind of exotic science fiction. Finally, in 1967, largely through the efforts of Robert Kennedy to publicize Indian problems, the large foundations decided to fund Indian programs. Ford, Carnegie, and Donner rushed into the field helter-skelter, eager to buy a few Indian projects.

In April of 1969, representatives of the thirty-six most prestigious foundations were sent invitations to attend a special conference on the problems of Hispanos, the second largest minority group in the nation. Almost universally they turned down the invitations. Mexicans were simply not within the thought-world of the large foundations. They had not yet related to Mexicans nor had Mexicans been able to attract their attention.

The result of the conference was that Vicente Ximenes, torn and discouraged, resigned his post as chairman of the federal Inter-Agency Committee on Mexican American Affairs. "We're just not that dumb, that's all; we're just not that dumb," Ximenes is reported to have said in disgust. Ximenes blamed the rejection on discrimination. He should have understood that until the foundations recognized that Mexicans were a part of American society they would get nothing because they were not a familiar item on the foundation agenda. There was no Mexican symbol in the foundation world.

A generation ago white children were taught to look directly at black people and pretend that they didn't realize that they were black. Viewing such behavior today with our experiences of the civil rights movement behind us, it appears to be the most unsophisticated and racist behavior imaginable. But *at the time* it was a sincere effort by an ignorant white populace who were truly concerned about equality to express equality by pretending that differences did not exist.

A comparable situation has long existed in the Indian community. The Indian name has always embarrassed the white man. They have tried to pretend that Running Bear, Black Feather, and Iron Shield are really good old-fashioned Anglo-Saxon names because *people* have Anglo-Saxon names. *Whites pretend* that Indian names are normal to them when they want to express the common humanity existing between red and white. When they are disdainful of Indians, they emphasize the strangeness of the Indian name.

On the Pine Ridge Indian reservation in South Dakota we had a visitor one year, a sympathetic Easterner who loved Indians. For days he tried to call Mr. White Rabbitt, an old full-blood, "Mr. Rabbitt," as if his name was Rabbitt and his first name was "white." Finally he gave up and said nothing, hiding his confusion and obvious embarrassment at the thought that anyone could be called White Rabbitt. In his anxiety to treat the Sioux as real people when they had never been within his thought-world before, he related everything to his criteria. In an unguarded moment he blew the whole scheme. When he was leaving he proudly announced that he was delighted to have met "Mr. Bunny Rabbitt."

During my first year as director of the National Congress of American Indians, I went with two other Indians to see a certain Congressman's wife who had expressed a desire to become acquainted (and therefore well known) with Indians. Helen Schierback, a Lumbee, Imelda Schreiner, a Cheyenne River Sioux, and I went to the lady's house for tea. All through the afternoon she kept asking us for our names when she addressed us. As we were leaving we had to give her our names once again so that she could bid us good-bye. As we went out the door she thanked us for coming and profusely apologized for not remembering our names. "Indian names," she said, "are so peculiar and hard to remember."

It had completely escaped her that we all had European names. In her mind was the conception that all Indians had funny or difficult names, so her natural and unconscious reaction was to have immense difficulty remembering our names. Thus while American society has been very proud of its liberalism and maturity in understanding the world, it has not really understood the world or the people in it. Proclaiming the relativity of all things, Americans have carefully acted according to their own mythologies of the world.

By talking one way and acting in the opposite, we have tended to create conditions which are the exact reverse of what our goals tell us will happen. Morroe Berger gives a good example of how this happens in his book, *Equality by Statute*. He describes the black community's need for federal housing as it became apparent in the 1930s and 40s. In the Second World War, he points out, private industry built 56 percent of all housing for whites but only 14 percent of the housing for blacks. So the black community supported federal housing programs as a means of eliminating segregation in housing patterns. Government agencies adopted rules toward nondiscriminatory housing in the 1950s and massive housing programs were initiated in the slums to provide housing on a nondiscriminatory basis. The ultimate effect of such programs was discriminatory, however, although this was completely unintentional.

"The federal programs helped increase segregation in several ways," Berger writes. "By insuring mortgages for low-income families they helped to concentrate Negroes in the urban low-cost projects. By encouraging slum clearance, they threw many Negro families into even more segregated housing." The effort to provide a better housing pattern was thwarted by the failure to understand all the elements that were subject to change during the development of the plan. The vision of new housing was limited because the view of the problem was fragmented into component parts. When a unity of understanding was made possible, it was apparent that the program had not been successful in creating nondiscriminatory housing. It had intensified the problem.

A comparable policy in the field of Indian Affairs nearly destroyed Indians. In order to give Indian people opportunities for employment, a program of termination of federal responsibilities was initiated. Indians were forced into the cities on a program aptly called "relocation." Not only did the program fail to assimilate the people who went to the urban areas, it paralyzed those remaining on the reservations and resulted in a decade of stagnation for the Indian community at large. In those areas where the termination policy was successfully applied by Congress (the Menominee tribe of Wisconsin, the Klamath tribe of Oregon, the mixed-blood Utes of Utah, and the scattered bands of western Oregon), the condition of the people rapidly deteriorated without federal support. A program purporting to provide opportunities resulted in their denial.

McLuhan remarks that "not only have backward and nonindustrial cultures no specialist habits to overcome in their encounter with electromagnetism but they still have much of their traditional oral culture that has the total unified 'field' character of our new electromagnetism. Our old industrial areas, having eroded their oral traditions automatically, are in the position of having to rediscover them in order to cope with the electric age."

The collapse of traditional industrial mythology which has created the collective amnesia is a phenomenon of the electric universe. In talking of the speed of communications, McLuhan observes that "a very much greater speed-up, such as occurs with electricity, may serve to restore a tribal pattern of intense involvement such as took place with the introduction of radio in Europe, and is now tending to happen as a result of TV in America. Specialist technologies detribalize. The nonspecialist electric technology retribalizes."

Whether we like it or not we are today in the midst of a process of retribalization. Like the tribesmen who were our ancestors, we have become objects of a universe we do not understand and not subjects with a universe to exploit. By our technology we have reversed the traditional religious and political thinking concerning man as the master of his own fate. Instead of an arbitrary nature we have come to fear an arbitrary technology, an impartial and inhuman science.

If the nature of our electric world is that it retribalizes, then we must begin to create a new mythology and symbols to explain that world. New concepts must define the questions of life, death, and society which are derived from the nature of man as a tribal animal. The individualistic rationalism that has brought Western man to the present cannot preserve his sanity for him in the future.

We have come from an oral culture through a literate culture and then suddenly been thrust beyond the literate culture by our communications media into a qualitatively different oral culture again. This generation of young people has been raised on television and has lived a continuous existence instead of the broken and alienated existence which plagued their elders. The categories of existence are different for the generations and the older generation cannot stand the freedom which the young exhibit.

The emergence of the Woodstock Nation as a distinct minority group underlines the basic conflict between the outlooks of the two generations. It was the logical conclusion for a young generation characterized by high suicide and automobile accident death rates. The power movements also indicate that the older mythology of equality of individuals, when it was not realized through civil rights legislation, was quickly rejected in favor of group tactics and goals.

What we desperately need now are transitional structures, concepts, and mythologies to provide a means of translating ideas and values between generations and between whites and non-whites. Communication has become oral and experiential. Feeling is a more important tool of analysis than a dictionary or encyclopedia. Groups provide a more accurate gauge of feelings than does individual evaluation. Thus the be-in and rock festival have become the important events of our time. If young people and minority groups are to survive the repression that we see today the harmless group feeling must be translated into the demand for recognition of the sovereignty of their groups. This can only come through political action as a defensive weapon of protection. Unless these groups quickly flex their muscles in a manner comprehensible to their opponents, they will be destroyed.

Any future coalition of groups for change must adopt Indian formats. The desire to have spectacular demonstrations and disruptions must give way to a determination to maintain the community at all costs. This can only be possible by creation of new mythologies internal to each group in a manner similar to contemporary tribal understandings of the history of the people. While McLuhan looks for the industrial society to regain its old forms he cannot also help but see that this will require disintegration before fragments are able to integrate themselves around new centers.

As we see contemporary society we see the world at the moment of creation. We have the chance to build a new cosmopolitan society within the older American society. But it must be done by an affirmation of the component groups that have composed American society. We can no longer build upon a denial of everything that makes a person himself. The communications gap is a vast chasm at the bottom of which flows a swift river. By renewing various symbols we can begin a pontoon bridge for the eventual restoration of communication from shore to shore. But a simple renewal of symbolism has already been tried with little success. It has failed because it has been tried with tactics derived from an older age.

We cannot review the past without understanding that symbols and the tactics used to communicate them depend upon a new vision of the nature of man. This can only be possible by creating a new mythology of creation itself. The current fascination with ecology is one key to the new mythology because it attempts to understand the real natural world as a part of us and we as a part of it. The key to the communications gap is thus really quite simple. We must return to and understand the land we occupy. Communications have made the continent a part of the global village. The process must be reversed. The land must now define the role communications can play to make the country fruitful again.

2 * STEREOTYPING

One reason that Indian people have not been heard from until recently is that we have been completely covered up by movie Indians. Western movies have been such favorites that they have dominated the public's conception of what Indians are. It is not all bad when one thinks about the handsome Jay Silverheels bailing the Lone Ranger out of a jam, or Ed Ames rescuing Daniel Boone with some clever Indian trick. But the other mythologies that have wafted skyward because of the movies have blocked out any idea that there might be real Indians with real problems.

Other minority groups have fought tenaciously against stereotyping, and generally they have been successful. Italians quickly quashed the image of them as mobsters that television projected in *The Untouchables*. Blacks have been successful in getting a more realistic picture of the black man in a contemporary setting because they have had standout performers like Bill Cosby and Sidney Poitier to represent them.

Since stereotyping was highlighted by motion pictures, it would probably be well to review the images of minority groups projected in the movies in order to understand how the situation looks at present. Perhaps the first aspect of stereotyping was the tendency to exclude people on the basis of their inability to handle the English language. Not only were racial minorities excluded, but immigrants arriving on these shores were soon whipped into shape by ridicule of their English.

Traditional stereotypes pictured the black as a happy watermelon-eating darky whose sole contribution to American society was his indiscriminate substitution of the "d" sound for "th." Thus a black always said "dis" and "dat," as in "lift dat bale." The "d" sound carried over and was used by white gangsters to indicate disfavor with their situation, as in "dis is de end, ya rat." The important thing was to indicate that blacks were like lisping children not yet competent to undertake the rigors of economic opportunities and voting.

Mexicans were generally portrayed as shiftless and padded out for siesta, without any redeeming qualities whatsoever. Where the black had been handicapped by his use of the "d," the Mexican suffered from the use of the double "e." This marked them off as a group worth watching. Mexicans, according to the stereotype, always said "theenk," "peenk," and later "feenk." Many advertisements today still continue this stereotype, thinking that it is cute and cuddly.

These groups were much better off than Indians were. Indians were always devoid of any English whatsoever. They were only allowed to speak when an important message had to be transmitted on the screen. For example, "many pony soldiers die" was meant to indicate that Indians were going to attack the peaceful settlers who happened to have broken their three hundredth treaty moments before. Other than that Indian linguistic ability was limited to "ugh" and "kemo sabe" (which means honky in some obscure Indian language).

The next step was to acknowledge that there was a great American dream to which any child could aspire. (It was almost like the train in the night that Richard Nixon heard as a child anticipating the dream fairy.) The great American dream was projected in the early World War II movies. The last reel was devoted to a stirring proclamation that we were going to win the war and it showed factories producing airplanes, people building ships, and men marching in uniform to the transports. There was a quick pan of a black face before the scene shifted to scenes of orchards, rivers, Mount Rushmore, and the Liberty Bell as we found out what we were fighting for.

The new images expressed a profound inability to understand why minority groups couldn't "make it" when everybody knew what America was all about—freedom and equality. By projecting an image of everyone working hard to win the war, the doctrine was spread that America was just one big happy family and that there really weren't any differences so long as we had to win the war.

It was a rare war movie in the 1940s that actually showed a black or a Mexican as a bona fide fighting man. When they did appear it was in the role of cooks or orderlies serving whites. In most cases this was a fairly accurate statement of their situation, particularly with respect to the Navy.

World War II movies were entirely different for Indians. Each platoon of red-blooded white American boys was equipped with its own set of Indians. When the platoon got into trouble and was surrounded, its communications cut off except for one slender line to regimental headquarters, and that line tapped by myriads of Germans, Japanese, or Italians, the stage was set for the dramatic episode of the Indians.

John Wayne, Randolph Scott, Sonny Tufts, or Tyrone Power would smile broadly as he played his ace, which until this time had been hidden from view. From nowhere, a Navajo, Comanche, Cherokee, or Sioux would appear, take the telephone, and in some short and inscrutable phraseology communicate such a plenitude of knowledge to his fellow tribesman (fortunately situated at the general's right hand) that fighting units thousands of miles away would instantly perceive the situation and rescue the platoon. The Indian would disappear as mysteriously as he had come, only to reappear the next week in a different battle to perform his esoteric rites. Anyone watching war movies during the 40s would have been convinced that without Indian telephone operators the war would have been lost irretrievably, in spite of John Wayne.

Indians were America's secret weapon against the forces of evil. The typing spoke of a primitive gimmick, and it was the strangeness of Indians that made them visible, not their humanity. With the Korean War era and movies made during the middle 50s, other minority groups began to appear and Indians were pushed into the background. This era was the heyday of the "All-American Platoon." It was the ultimate conception of intergroup relations. The "All-American Platoon" was a "one each": one black, one Mexican, one Indian, one farm boy from Iowa, one Southerner who hated blacks, one boy from Brooklyn, one Polish boy from the urban slums of the Midwest, one Jewish intellectual, and one college boy. Every possible stereotype was included and it resulted in a portrayal of Indians as another species of human being for the first time in moving pictures.

The platoon was always commanded by a veteran of grizzled countenance who had been at every battle in which the United States had ever engaged. The whole story consisted in killing off the members of the platoon until only the veteran and the college boy were left. The Southerner and the black would die in each other's arms singing "Dixie." The Jewish intellectual and the Indian formed some kind of attachment and were curiously the last ones killed. When the smoke cleared, the college boy, with a prestige wound in the shoulder, returned to his girl, and the veteran reconciled with his wife and checked out another platoon in anticipation of taking the same hill in the next movie.

While other groups have managed to make great strides since those days, Indians have remained the primitive unknown quantity. Dialogue has reverted back to the monosyllabic grunt and even pictures that attempt to present the Indian side of the story depend upon unintelligible noises to present their message. The only exception to this rule is a line famed for its durability over the years. If you fall asleep during the Late Show and suddenly awaken to the words "go in peace my son," it is either an Indian chief bidding his son good-bye as the boy heads for college or a Roman Catholic priest forgiving Paul Newman or Steve McQueen for killing a hundred men in the preceding reel.

Anyone raising questions about the image of minority groups as portrayed in television and the movies is automatically suspect as an un-American and subversive influence on the minds of the young. The historical, linguistic, and cultural differences are neatly blocked out by the fad of portraying members of minority groups in roles which formerly were reserved for whites. Thus Burt Reynolds played a Mohawk detective busy solving the crime problem in New York City. Diahann Carroll played a well-to-do black widow with small child in a television series that was obviously patterned after the unique single-headed white family.

In recent years the documentary has arisen to present the story of Indian people and a number of series on Black America have been produced. Indian documentaries are singularly the same. A reporter and television crew hasten to either the Navajo or Pine

Ridge reservation, quickly shoot reels on poverty conditions, and return East blithely thinking that they have captured the essence of Indian life. In spite of the best intentions, the eternal yearning to present an exciting story of a strange people overcomes, and the endless cycle of poverty-oriented films continues.

This type of approach continually categorizes the Indian as an incompetent boob who can't seem to get along and who is hopelessly mired in a poverty of his own making. Hidden beneath these documentaries is the message that Indians really WANT to live this way. No one has yet filmed the incredible progress that is being made by the Makah tribe, the Quinaults, Red Lake Chippewas, Gila River Pima-Maricopas, and others. Documentaries project the feeling that reservations should be eliminated because the conditions are so bad. There is no effort to present the bright side of Indian life.

With the rise of ethnic studies programs and courses in minority-group history, the situation has become worse. People who support these programs assume that by communicating the best aspects of a group they have somehow solved the major problems of that group in its relations with the rest of society. By emphasizing that black is beautiful or that Indians have contributed the names of rivers to the road map, many people feel that they have done justice to the group concerned.

One theory of interpretation of Indian history that has arisen in the past several years is that all of the Indian war chiefs were patriots defending their lands. This is the "patriot chief" interpretation of history. Fundamentally it is a good theory in that it places a more equal balance to interpreting certain Indian wars as wars of resistance. It gets away from the tendency, seen earlier in this century, to classify all Indian warriors as renegades. But there is a tendency to overlook the obvious renegades, Indians who were treacherous and would have been renegades had there been no whites to fight. The patriot chiefs interpretation also conveniently overlooks the fact that every significant leader of the previous century was eventually done in by his own people in one way or another. Sitting Bull was killed by Indian police working for the government. Geronimo was captured by an army led by Apache scouts who sided with the United States.

If the weak points of each minority group's history are to be covered over by a sweetness-and-light interpretation based on what we would like to think happened rather than what did happen, we doom ourselves to decades of further racial strife. Most of the study programs today emphasize the goodness that is inherent in the different minority communities, instead of trying to present a balanced story. There are basically two schools of interpretation running through all of these efforts as the demand for black, red, and brown pride dominates the programs.

One theory derives from the "All-American Platoon" concept of a decade ago. Under this theory members of the respective racial minority groups had an important role in the great events of American history. Crispus Attucks, a black, almost single-handedly started the Revolutionary War, while Eli Parker, the Seneca Indian general, won the Civil War and would have concluded it sooner had not there been so many stupid whites abroad in those days. This is the "cameo" theory of history. It takes a basic "manifest destiny" white interpretation of history and lovingly plugs a few feathers, woolly heads, and sombreros into the famous events of American history. No one tries to explain what an Indian is who was helping the whites destroy his own people, since we are now all Americans and have these great events in common.

The absurdity of the cameo school of ethnic pride is self-apparent. Little Mexican children are taught that there were some good Mexicans at the Alamo. They can therefore be happy that Mexicans have been involved in the significant events of Texas history.

Little is said about the Mexicans on the other side at the Alamo. The result is a denial of a substantial Mexican heritage by creating the feeling that "we all did it together." If this trend continues I would not be surprised to discover that Columbus had a Cherokee on board when he set sail from Spain in search of the Indies.

The cameo school smothers any differences that existed historically by presenting a history in which all groups have participated through representatives. Regardless of Crispus Attuck's valiant behavior during the Revolution, it is doubtful that he envisioned another century of slavery for blacks as a cause worth defending.

The other basic school of interpretation is a projection backward of the material blessings of the white middle class. It seeks to identify where all the material wealth originated and finds that each minority group *contributed* something. It can therefore be called the contribution school. Under this conception we should all love Indians because they contributed corn, squash, potatoes, tobacco, coffee, rubber, and other agricultural products. In like manner, blacks and Mexicans are credited with Carver's work on the peanut, blood transfusion, and tacos and tamales.

The ludicrous implication of the contribution school visualizes the minority groups clamoring to enter American society, lined up with an abundance of foods and fancies, presenting them to whites in a never-ending stream of generosity. If the different minority groups were given an overriding 2 percent royalty on their contributions, the same way whites have managed to give themselves royalties for their inventions, this school would have a more realistic impact on minority groups.

The danger with both of these types of ethnic studies theories is that they present an unrealistic account of the role of minority groups in American history. Certainly there is more to the story of the American Indian than providing cocoa and popcorn for Columbus' landing party. When the clashes of history are smoothed over in favor of a mushy togetherness feeling, then people begin to wonder what has happened in the recent past that has created the conditions of today. It has been the feeling of younger people that contemporary problems have arisen because community leadership has been consistently betraying them. Older statesmen are called Uncle Toms, and the entire fabric of accumulated wisdom and experience of the older generation of minority groups is destroyed.

Rising against the simplistic cameo and contribution schools is the contemporary desire by church leaders to make Christianity relevant to minority groups by transposing the entire Christian myth and archetypes into Indian, black, and Mexican terms. Thus Father Groppi, noted white-black priest, wants to have black churches show a black Christ. This is absurd, because Christ was, as everyone knows, a Presbyterian, and he was a white man. That is to say, for nearly two thousand years he has been a white man. To suddenly show him as black, Mexican, or Indian takes away the whole meaning of the myth.

The Indian counterpart of the black Christ is the Christmas card portraying the Holy Family living in a hogan in Monument Valley on the Navajo reservation. As the shepherds sing and gather their flocks, little groups of Navajo angels announce the birth of the Christchild. The scene is totally patronizing and unrealistic. If the Christchild was born on the Navajo reservation, his chances of surviving the first two years of life would be less than those of the original Jesus with Herod chasing him. (We have not yet reached the point of showing three officials from the Bureau of Indian Affairs coming up the canyon as the Three Wise Men, but someone with a keen sense of relevancy will try it sooner or later.)

This type of religious paternalism overlooks the fact that the original figures of religious myths were designed to communicate doctrines. It satisfies itself by presenting its basic figures as so universalized that anyone can participate at any time in history. Thus the religion that it is trying to communicate becomes ahistorical, as Mickey Mouse and Snow White are ahistorical.

If the attempted renovation of religious imagery is ever combined with the dominant schools of ethnic studies, the result will be the Last Supper as the gathering of the "All-American Platoon" highlighted by the contributions of each group represented. Instead of simple bread and wine the table will be overflowing with pizza, tamales, greens, peanuts, popcorn, German sausage, and hamburgers. Everyone will feel that they have had a part in the creation of the great American Christian social order. Godless Communism will be vanquished.

Under present conceptions of ethnic studies there can be no lasting benefit either to minority groups or to society at large. The pride that can be built into children and youth by acknowledgment of the validity of their group certainly cannot be built by simply transferring symbols and interpretations arising in white cultural history into an Indian, black, or Mexican setting. The result will be to make the minority groups bear the white man's burden by using his symbols and stereotypes as if they were their own.

There must be a drive within each minority group to understand its own uniqueness. This can only be done by examining what experiences were relevant to the group, not what experiences of white America the group wishes itself to be represented in. As an example, the discovery of gold in California was a significant event in the experience of white America. The discovery itself was irrelevant to the western Indian tribes, but the migrations caused by the discovery of gold were vitally important. The two histories can dovetail around this topic but ultimately each interpretation must depend upon its orientation to the group involved.

What has been important and continues to be important is the Constitution of the United States and its continual adaptation to contemporary situations. With the Constitution as a framework and reference point, it would appear that a number of conflicting interpretations of the experience of America could be validly given. While they might conflict at every point as each group defines to its own satisfaction what its experience has meant, recognition that within the Constitutional framework we are engaged in a living process of intergroup relationships would mean that no one group could define the meaning of American society to the exclusion of any other.

Self-awareness of each group must define a series of histories about the American experience. Manifest destiny has dominated thinking in the past because it has had an abstract quality that appeared to interpret experiences accurately. Nearly every racial and ethnic group has had to bow down before this conception of history and conform to an understanding of the world that it did not ultimately believe. Martin Luther King, Jr., spoke to his people on the basis of self-awareness the night before he died. He told them that they as a people would reach the promised land. Without the same sense of destiny, minority groups will simply be adopting the outmoded forms of stereotyping by which whites have deluded themselves for centuries.

We can survive as a society if we reject the conquest-oriented interpretation of the Constitution. While some Indian nationalists want the whole country back, a guarantee of adequate protection of existing treaty rights would provide a meaningful compromise. The Constitution should provide a sense of balance between groups as it has between conflicting desires of individuals.

As each group defines the ideas and doctrines necessary to

maintain its own sense of dignity and identity, similarities in goals can be drawn that will have relevance beyond immediate group aspirations. Stereotyping will change radically because the ideological basis for portraying the members of any group will depend on that group's values. Plots in books and movies will have to show life as it is seen from within the group. Society will become broader and more cosmopolitan as innovative themes are presented to it. The universal sense of inhumanity will take on an aspect of concreteness. From the variety of cultural behavior patterns we can devise a new understanding of humanity.

The problem of stereotyping is not so much a racial problem as it is a problem of limited knowledge and perspective. Even though minority groups have suffered in the past by ridiculous characterizations of themselves by white society, they must not fall into the same trap by simply reversing the process that has stereotyped them. Minority groups must thrust through the rhetorical blockade by creating within themselves a sense of "peoplehood." This ultimately means the creation of a new history and not mere amendments to the historical interpretations of white America.

3 * TACTICS OR STRATEGY?

DURING THE RISE of the civil rights movement and its expansion into the power movements, Indian people were often derided for their refusal to participate in demonstrations and confrontations. Every time an activist discovered Indians, he was horrified to learn that they were not about to begin marching. Because they equated Indian problems with those of other groups, many people felt that if Indians used the same tactics which had worked with the black community, Indian problems could be solved. Everyone spoke of the spectacular results that other groups were having, and it became sociological heresy for Indians to refuse to imitate these other groups.

As resistance to the Vietnam War grew, demonstrations and protests became commonplace. Although Indians may have silently disliked the war, there was little inclination to follow the tactics of others to raise the issue. With the exception of a few characters bought and paid for by liberal church and New Left funds, there has been remarkably little outward indication that Indians were upset about anything, even though a massive shift in thought, now characterized as the Red Power movement, was spreading through Indian country.

In the decade of the 60s Indian people made tremendous progress. If measured on a per capita basis in funds, it would be far in excess of the progress made by other groups. In some instances official policy affecting Indian lives and property was vitally changed. The Vice-President's Council on Indian Opportunity, for example, a multidepartment council for coordinating Indian programs, was set up early in 1968 and has been functioning on a high level to keep the spotlight on Indian problems.

One reason why Indians have been silent, and yet making good progress, is that they have refused to become wedded to one tactic. Instead, tribal leaders have adopted an overall sense of strategy that views all problems over a span of time. There has therefore been no sense of urgency to impel the continued use of certain tactics.

In general, antiwar groups have been shortsighted and have used one type of tactic to the exclusion of others. They have consequently exhausted themselves, confused the nation, and created shifts in policy which they had not contemplated. The most effective drive against the Vietnam War was the campaign through the snows of New Hampshire in 1968 on behalf of Senator Eugene McCarthy. It provided the momentum by which dissent was expressed unequivocally, for it registered the fact that sufficient organization might defeat certain hawks in the coming elections. Everyone heard that message.

On the other hand, the self-immolations, the burnings of American flags, and the obscenities used to express disgust with American foreign policy fundamentally created a super-hawk situation which produced some 9½ million votes for George Wallace and drove the Democrats out in favor of the colorless and inept Republicans. It would be fair to say that in spite of the enthusiasm and sacrifice of the antiwar people, they did not realize the extent to which television was transforming their symbolic protests to communicate a different message to the public at large. There was and is a need for an examination of the tactics which have been used as communicative devices in line with the basic philosophical implications of the electric age.

At present, people are bewildered by the massive dislocations in the social structure. A demonstration can hardly begin before it is transmitted coast to coast by the communications media. Television is caught between the accusation that it encourages demonstrations and the reply that it is merely reporting them. The inability to transcend this conflict of defining the role of media in triggering and reporting events has been responsible for the rise in irrational fear experienced by our society. The result has been Congressional hearings into television violence and the censoring of the Smothers Brothers.

A restricted thought and value structure in which people are able to understand events has resulted in a repressive method of reacting to the events. Thus the right wing has been more than willing to loose troops on people with no more excuse than that property might be in danger or that order is not being maintained. The moral and symbolic issues cannot be raised in the present context of demonstrations since the demonstrations themselves have been communicated, not the symbolism behind them. For this reason the last gigantic moratorium against the Vietnam War in November of 1969 fell flat and resulted in the virtual dissolution of the antiwar front.

Every event of the past two decades which has had extensive television coverage has been emotionally evaluated by the viewers in terms of their own experiences. Long after the fact, official explanations have dwindled down from official channels indicating that the government has not really understood the issue. This time gap between events and official explanations of what those events meant created the civil rights movement. While the audience saw blacks brutalized and suffered with them, tempers rose. Then official explanations by Southern sheriffs that they had to maintain law and order against violent demonstrators (who were often school children praying) simply did not hold water and raised the hackles of the general public.

One of the classic techniques of the early civil rights movement was to engage in peaceful demonstrations with the certain knowledge that the Southern establishment would lose its cool and react with violence, thus communicating the very issue that needed to be communicated. Martin Luther King, Jr., in his book *Where Do We Go From Here: Chaos or Community?*, relates that the successful strategy of the early days was "unconsciously patterned [for] a crisis policy and program, and summoned support not for daily commitment but for explosive events alone."

In calling for massive support on certain legislation, the blacks in reality asked only for the warm bodies of whites to parade with them protesting the evil under attack in a certain crisis situation. The real message that was communicated to the white community by black leadership was that passage of certain legislation would bring the civil rights issues to solution. This white America did. It got the laws passed.

When Martin Luther King, Jr., complained about the liberal attitude that "the recording of the law in itself is treated as the reality of the reform," he failed to realize that this message was all that had been asked of white America. Passing certain pieces of legislation raised only an ethical dilemma, and this dilemma was solved when the legislation was passed. Feeling that "every ethical appeal to the conscience of the white man must be accomplished by nonviolent pressure," King, through reliance on the demonstration as the medium by which the message was transmitted, simply raised a number of ethical questions which could be answered by legislative means but did not in fact raise the necessary moral issues which would guarantee white support without demonstrations.

In this aspect Barry Goldwater was correct: you cannot legislate moral behavior. Insofar as the black community was able to raise issues of ethical content, it was able to move the nation forward in the area of civil rights. Yet the conservative elements fell back on the argument of ultimate morality and refused to budge, either to allow the temporary validity of the ethical questions raised by the black community or to themselves assume the responsibility for the ultimate moral issue. Thus the technique of demonstrations and confrontations continued on its way, although steadily losing its novelty as a media of communication.

Thus King said of his technique: "Sound effort in a single city such as Birmingham or Selma produced situations that symbolized the evil everywhere and inflamed public opinion against it. Where the spotlight illuminated the evil, a legislative remedy was soon obtained that applied everywhere." As creator of symbolic events, King was a genius, but as the symbol faded he still continued to use the same techniques. His movement was built upon crisis, and it could not fall back into a slower time sequence without losing its effectiveness and apparent progressive motion forward.

The disastrous activity of Hubert Humphrey at the 1964 Democratic Convention resulted in the death of symbolic alliances between black and white. Faced with the choice of seating the Mississippi Freedom Democratic Party or the regulars who had systematically excluded blacks from participation in the state party, Humphrey opted for the Vice-Presidency and advocated a symbolic compromise victory for the blacks by giving them a token delegation.

It was the wrong act by the wrong man at the wrong time. Humphrey had a sterling record of commitment to civil rights causes, ripping apart the 1948 convention by his insistence on a strong civil rights plank. In January of 1964 Humphrey had come within a whisker of getting total Indian support for the civil rights bill of that year. He had every reason to push through the seating of the MFDP and cement the minority communities and the Democratic Party for another generation. He would have solidified the support of militant white youths looking to their elders for morality.

But Humphrey preferred to play it as safe as possible and he worked to satisfy the old order which had no possibility of understanding the changes that were taking place around them in Mississippi. In doing so he insulted the intelligence of the younger generation which had assumed, up to that point, that Humphrey was committed to the morality of civil rights.

Stokely Carmichael recorded his feelings as to the Humphrey compromise in *Black Power*:

> The two MFDP delegates were not to be seated as representatives. Supposedly, the two guest seats were "of great symbolic value." But the MFDP did not go to the Convention as a symbolic act; it went in a sincere effort to become part of the national Democratic party.

Humphrey blew it for his party, for America, and for the future of intergroup relations when he failed to understand the desire of the Mississippi Freedom Democratic Party. From that point on, the liberals were suspect, and people began to realize that the liberals might be committed more to remaining in power than to solving problems. This suspicion was fully realized by Humphrey's activity at the convention of 1968, when he failed to comprehend what was happening outside his hotel room. Humphrey, the most noted liberal of our day, killed the liberal image as the great symbol of shelter against oppression when he watched the roll call elect him as the Democratic standard bearer amidst the brutality of Chicago.

The symbolic act is dead. It could be resurrected only by a completely new mythology in which the impact of communications media and the death of traditional symbology is taken seriously. The 1964 Democratic Convention may have been the last time a symbolic act was offered and rejected between the generations. Yet there has been no acknowledgment by liberals, churches, or people in general indicating they understand that the old symbolic world is dead.

Liberals crowed about the ability of Eugene McCarthy to get youth involved in the political process, as if their generation had pulled a coup over the immature youth. Yet there is every indication that youth used McCarthy as a vehicle to express their views. Notably, he was unable to transfer any of his attraction and influence over youth to Humphrey when he finally did endorse Humphrey in 1968.

The "police riot" at Chicago showed how effective and dangerous youth had really become. They had raised issues which could not be solved by symbolic acts or acts of apparent contrition. The traditional mythology of American philosophy—individualism and rationalism—upon which the political processes were built, was shaken and nearly tumbled. Had the liberals had more backbone and understanding, they might have rejected the symbolism of the Humphrey candidacy and swept the convention and the election. But they did little more than respond to the media of youth and march in sympathy to show their solidarity with the youth, then retired licking their wounds.

In almost every area of life the symbology of previous days has worn out and is showing its barrenness. Professor Harold Mendelsohn, addressing a convention of Colorado Democrats in March of 1969, said that the political parties are strangling on their own mythology, that the political campaign of today is a "pseudo-event," and that the entire process from FDR through JFK was to package a personal image and call it "Democratic." When Richard Nixon created the "new Nixon," he in effect created an entity which would and could change to reflect everything that was bothering voters without actually facing any of the ultimate issues. Mendelsohn also predicted the end of political parties as a viable expression of the members.

One of the cases settled by the Supreme Court in 1969 concerned the wearing of black armbands in school as a protest against the Vietnam War. Although the Court supported the wearing of armbands as "symbolic speech," Justice Hugo Black's dissent is worthy of note. As the school officials predicted, the wearing of armbands did distract the students from their studies. "If," Justice Black wrote, "the time has come when pupils of state-supported schools, kindergartens, grammar schools, or high schools, can defy and flaunt orders of school officials to keep their minds on their own school work, it is the beginning of a new revolutionary era of permissiveness in this country fostered by the judiciary."

Black was correct that this was the ultimate message transmitted by the upholding of the symbolic speech represented by the armbands. Without a new context in which such behavior made sense, and in which, indeed, not to wear armbands would have been strange, the traditional methods of interpretation made it seem as if the Supreme Court was creating an era of extreme permissiveness. Unless society can pierce traditional mythological interpretations of behavior, it must be prepared to come to a final division between those people who can and those people who cannot use the communications media to understand the events of life.

Government policies often reflect the symbology of one age conflicting with the increasing awareness of change. Most flagrant of these conflicts is the policy on tobacco. The Public Health Service reflecting the new knowledge achieved in our recent experience is devoted to denouncing cigarettes as harmful to health. But the Agricultural Department, in the three years ending in 1968, spent $61.5 million to subsidize exports of tobacco, $9.5 million in price supports, and $69.3 million in tobacco disposed of as foreign aid for foreign countries and which could not be converted into dollars. The federal government, as of March 1969, had some $750 million invested in tobacco in warehouses. In this case the symbols of health and economic support are "*mutually exclusive*." They have no common reference point whatsoever. The need for a new mythology and symbology to encompass two contradictory policies and symbols is apparent.

Equally as silly and futile is the quarrel between educators and students over the policies of the universities. In the spring of 1969 the University of Colorado culminated its longstanding fight against the local SDS chapter by disaffiliating. The penalty of disaffiliation was regarded as largely a "symbolic" matter, that is to say, in the University of Colorado context, it meant exactly nothing. Affiliation gave only a few privileges and the SDS did not lose all of those. One dean is reported to have said that disaffiliation was a "sop to the public" which had been demanding action.

One official said that disaffiliation meant that legally the SDS could not call themselves the Colorado University chapter, but later admitted that the university probably couldn't do anything about it if they did decide to call themselves the Colorado University Chapter of SDS. In short, the traditional symbols of authority—affiliation or disaffiliation—had been worn out, and nobody knew what to do without the reality of symbolic recognition by the university.

Again, in the Nixon position on integration in the South, the inability of symbolism to communicate issues was painfully apparent. Nixon was supported in the South because of his implicit promise to stop integration plans of the federal government. By dropping the Johnson Administration guidelines and deadlines for integration, the Nixon Administration appeared to be fulfilling its promise to the South. But at the same time it was trying to assure the Northern liberals and the black community that the relaxation of guidelines was in no way compromising the federal government to Southerners. Hence the symbol became a betrayal to both sections of the nation, and it is doubtful whether the real situation will ever be understood by either the public or the administration.

In 1968, the students made Columbia University a byword for revolution and discontent. When the SDS tried to duplicate the feat in May of 1969, it fell flat, and one student was heard to remark that "it's useless to pretend you're launching an enormous struggle when no one is there to support you." In the period of a year, the students of Columbia had decided that the medium of taking over buildings really had nothing to do with communicating the just demands of the students. At least at Columbia, that medium became unable to transmit the message and was dropped.

In the same manner, sentences for draft resistance did not have the slightest effect in deterring resistance. Selective Service laws are now the third or fourth most frequently broken federal statutes. As of April, 1969, some 2,200 draft cases were awaiting trial in spite of the fact that they had priority on federal criminal dockets. Traditional symbols of flexibility and repression, the halt in bombing and the prosecution of Dr. Spock, did not have the slightest effect on the resistance. Students and youth had simply chosen to fight it out on certain grounds and were acting in accordance with their convictions. The symbol of the draft resister had taken on a moral and honorable status. It would have been regarded as traitorous two decades earlier. The students have converted the symbol from one generation's negative value concept to their own generation's positive value concept.

Even before Teddy Kennedy had his future abridged in Chappaquiddick, serious questions were being raised as to the Kennedy symbol. In April, Kennedy led an expedition to Alaska to view the natives. The visit had hardly commenced before three Republican Senators announced that they felt it was a publicity buildup designed to boost Kennedy's chances for the 1972 Democratic nomination and that the natives were of minor importance. Senator George Murphy, experienced in publicity and communications techniques, was reported to have said that the trip was like sending advance men into town to promote a picture. Foremost in the controversy was a staff recommendation that the photographers and television cameras contrast native poverty and the affluence of government employees. The idea of contrasting images made the medium of the trip to investigate a "stage-managed scenario" according to one Senator.

The continuing war against marijuana is yet another example where the traditional bears no relationship to the realities of today. In June of 1969 the chairman of the National Science Foundation said that there is no real evidence that smoking marijuana is harmful or addictive. Some studies have shown, in fact, that marijuana may have less effect on driving ability than the nectar of the older generation, alcohol. The continual conflict over marijuana comes from the fact that it has a negative symbolism for the older generation and a positive symbolism for much of the younger generation. Since it is actually no better or worse than alcohol, and less damaging physically than tobacco, its danger lies primarily in that it symbolizes for the older generation a type of sexual and ethical behavior which they have been taught to reject.

Foremost in the manipulation of images has been Richard Nixon, particularly during the 1968 Presidential campaign. We have seen an almost continual mixing of political symbols from the Nixon Administration, so that it becomes impossible for people to understand what is policy and what is political payoff. The saving grace for the Republicans is that they have moved so slowly on every front that they have raised few expectations, and thus any movement appears to be one of significant involvement in the issues of the day.

The conflict of today is best exemplified in the trial of the Catonsville Nine for burning draft-board files in Catonsville, Maryland. The brilliant defense of the nine by William Kunstler was highlighted by an appeal to the morality of the case. But the defense showed that it had not reckoned with the message that was actually transmitted by the act.

The U.S. Attorney for Maryland, Stephen Sachs, prosecutor for the government, said that "what they did was, in principle, exactly what a lynch mob does. They arrogantly took the law into their own hands. Their act was *something more than symbolic.*" Again, in the Kunstler defense of the Milwaukee Fourteen, in spite of an appeal to the moral issue in the symbol of burning draft-board records, the state of Wisconsin refused to drop its charges. The assistant district attorney insisted that Wisconsin was prosecuting for theft, burglary, and arson, which are not political crimes. Again, the symbolism was lost and the message was the medium—theft, burglary, and arson.

It would seem, therefore, that unless a new philosophy of

human rights, a new universe of symbols, a new metaphysic of modern communication and values is devised, the conflict between segments of society will escalate with increasing seriousness. If we are to push beyond the barriers which face us in communication we must face the reality of symbolism. Symbols have disappeared because the medium has become the message. Things are what they appear to be in the most simplistic terms in the electric age.

When we introduce the idea of timing, then the problem becomes more than a choice of tactics, it becomes one primarily of thoughtful strategy and planning in which tactical options are opened and closed according to the situation which presents itself. Thus the basic task of leadership in minority groups and within that portion of the white community which allies itself with the concerns of minority groups is thoughtful analysis of every area in which problems are present. Surveying as broad a field as possible provides the basic data from which strategy can be formed. In essence, strategy then depends upon adequate and in-depth knowledge of the nature and problems of the respective minority groups.

The concentration upon ethnic studies can probably form one component of the development of strategy, since it will provide the historical background from which contemporary problems issue. But concentration solely upon the past will not suffice to provide a basic framework of interpretation by which present events can be understood, nor will it provide live options for the future. Each ethnic group must, in effect, form its own interpretation of itself from which it can choose those paths of action which can best be achieved within a certain time span. In this manner, the frictions and fears created by attacks on generalities can be avoided, and progress of perceptible note can be achieved.

Over the past decade Indian people have followed this pattern with some success, although they have not defined it as a technique which they were deliberately using, since it was developed internally and never became a slogan from which revolutionary fires could be kindled. The basic approach has been to interrelate problems, so that if progress could not be made in one area, frustrations would not build up but would be directed toward other tasks, and overall progress could be made. Indians have not allowed themselves to be ultimately diverted from a comprehensive overview of their situation, and they have been able to relate diverse problems to the basic integrity of the perpetuation of the tribe.

When a problem is defined as a lack of education, Indian people have balanced it off with demands for programs for housing and economic development. Waiting until education began to loosen up, they concentrated on economic development, hunting and fishing, or law and order problems, so that wherever a breakthrough occurred, they were ready to explore whatever progress could be made. When channels clogged up, energy was transferred to other fields, so that the pressure placed against the Bureau of Indian Affairs and related agencies remained a constant factor, although expressed in different ways and apparently unrelated in design.

Many tribes had wanted Congressional approval of a revolving loan fund in order to develop social-action programs; denied these funds, they applied themselves to other tasks until the funds from the war on poverty allowed them to release the frustrations with a sudden expansion of programs while the funding lasted. In this way progress was being made on many fronts, and the single-issue failures did not create an impasse within the tribal councils.

In 1964, the programs for preschool children of the Ute tribe in Utah were extremely popular and well regarded by other tribes. Had the war on poverty not come along, many tribes would have probably initiated similar programs similar to those of the Utes to assist their small children in educational programs. This would have meant a temporary diversion of funds to education from land programs or economic development, but as the pendulum swung back and forth the tribes would have been able to follow the trend and adjust quickly to the situation without being disrupted.

Basic to the technique of strategy has been the refusal of tribes to take the priority system very seriously. Early in the 1960s, the Department of the Interior began to develop ten-year Overall Economic Development Plans. Had the tribes followed the logic developed by Interior personnel, many of them would have collapsed completely, since the plans were basically foreign to the tribes. But with amazing agility and presence the tribes shifted whatever was possible at the time and ended up achieving a great many things out of the sequence in which they were planned.

Over the years the tribes have moved from a position in which they were not even allowed to handle their own funds to the status of contractors and subcontractors of basic services and surveys. All of this was done by maintaining a constant pressure in many areas of life and moving when there was a chance to move.

However, this technique has not been without its faults. Too many times Indian people have joined a movement only to see if there is a possibility, no matter how remote, of bringing the resources of the movement to bear on basic tribal problems. Thus many times tribes have made foolish moves and wasted funds which might otherwise have been invested in better projects. But these failures can be attributed largely to an inability to elaborate on the basic Indian viewpoint so that the implications of certain programs can be realized before any action is undertaken and the risks avoided.

When people have tried to understand the primary goals of the

Indian community it has proven literally impossible, since the national organizations, particularly the National Congress of American Indians, seem to pass the same resolutions year after year after year. For fourteen years the annual convention of the NCAI would return a resolution against P.L. 280 of the 83rd Congress, which gave the states unilateral jurisdiction over the civil and criminal affairs of the reservations. Finally, in 1968, they got the law amended and that concluded the struggle over state jurisdiction while the battle over other topics continued unabated.

The struggle over the area offices of the Bureau of Indian Affairs has gone on for at least a decade. Every meeting between tribes and Bureau officials contains elements of that struggle as the tribes continue to press for more authority in the agency offices and less in the area offices, in effect gutting the status of the area office by default. Eventually the tribes will wear the Interior Department down and eliminate the area offices, or they will have placed so much continual pressure on the area offices that they will have adapted them to a useful function.

In looking at the resolutions passed by Indian people, at their speeches given at regional meetings, and at the concerns they have had, one might extract the basic strategy of the tribes. In effect the tribes are pressing for complete independence from federal domination while retaining the maximum federal protection of the land base and services. With that goal, tribes shift back and forth to take advantage of every opportunity. The strategy has been to hit at every weak point that would yield more power to the tribe in the basic search for independence, and to surrender certain powers where it was possible to give them up without losing any momentum in the basic movement.

The Cheyenne River Sioux have been remarkably successful in maintaining a careful balance between taking and giving up of tribal powers and programs so that the general direction of tribal progress has been upward. No other tribe has made the progress which has been made at Cheyenne River over the last generation. While the tribe still has fundamental problems of a serious nature which will not be resolved in the near future, it in effect calls the shots on the reservation and outlines the avenues which will be used in the future.

When we speak of the future of intergroup relations in American society, we must speak somewhat in terms which tribes have been using, rather than in terms of generalities which tend to divide rather than to solve problems. Thus to speak of white racism does little but inflame tempers and create more heat than light. Whites are probably no more racist than any of the minority groups, but they just happen to have control of the structure of government at the present and their racism is strongly highlighted by those who are oppressed.

Would America be any better off if Indians, blacks, or Mexicans had control of it? The tempo would be much slower with Indians, probably much more poetic with blacks, and more romantic with Mexicans. But absolute power can corrupt any group of people, and so it is naïve to believe that any one group could do better than another in all respects.

What should be done at present is to form new understandings of how the American system works and what can be done to upgrade the social and political structure to make it function more immediately on problems of concern to people in general. Those who want to destroy the basic system with the delusion that they can create a better system simply do not understand systems at all. Also, they forget that revolutions tend to consume their creators, leaving the situation sometimes worse than the original problem. When one considers that the American Revolution was designed to escape unjust taxation, and when one then considers the state of taxation in this nation at present, the message should be clear.

Within the framework of the American system, then, immense

changes can be brought about which will be educational as well as progressive, which will prove constructive as well as creative, and which will cause people to think about the issues to be presented far more eloquently than will the dramatic but impotent gestures which have hitherto taken place. When one considers the impact of the McCarthy campaign on American politics and the radical changes which it has set in motion, it would seem that minority groups, progressives from both parties, youth, and all people who desire change and justice could sit down and contemplate the changes which might be made simply using the system as it is.

Few people can avoid the obvious message of George Wallace during the 1968 Presidential campaign. Wallace frankly stated that he was going to try to throw the election into the House of Representatives by taking enough electoral votes away from the two major-party candidates to prevent either one from winning a majority. The fact that he failed is not as significant as the fact that he, apparently representing the frantic right wing, was willing to work within the system and accept its judgment on his movement.

In contrast, the liberals and left-wing element pouted throughout the year, attaching themselves first to McCarthy and then to Kennedy, eventually deciding to create havoc in Chicago as a symbolic act of protest against the policies of the Democratic Administration. The New Left concluded the year by electing Nixon in place of Humphrey, who would have been much more amenable to their ideas, by having the South call the appointments within the Nixon Administration, and by having the very real possibility within the decade of having a violently right-wing Supreme Court which would drastically reduce individual rights in favor of strict civil order.

Few people in the New Left movement understood the significance of the national conventions. Neither Humphrey or Nixon carried New York or California delegations on the convention floor. Each state delegation in each party very definitely wanted someone else to head the ticket. It goes without saying, then, that New York and California went to Humphrey and Nixon, respectively, by default.

Suppose the New Left, instead of creating the havoc it did, had formed a new political party for that one campaign only. The party would have run in only New York and California and would have had as its ticket McCarthy and Lindsay. Suppose the students and dissidents who were disenchanted with both tickets had devoted their energy to those two states in overwhelming numbers, taking the time and energy to carefully present the issues and work in the local communities to bring out the voters who were sympathetic to their cause.

In those two states lay a total of 84 electoral votes. If the McCarthy-Lindsay ticket had taken those two states, it would have been sufficient to deny the Nixon ticket the victory, and the New Left would have been in a much more powerful position than George Wallace ever dreamed, when the House of Representatives gathered to elect the President.

Again, the symbolic Poor People's Campaign, which was designed to bring the fact of brutal and abject poverty to Congressional attention, dissolved into catcalls at Congressional windows and rejection in Congress of the demands of the participants. After all, when you have called someone a racist, what else can you call him?

With Congressional elections coming in the fall of 1968, minority groups and their friends might have done better to have chosen several notorious Congressional members who had consistently voted against progressive programs in each party. Then a concentrated effort should have been made in those Congressional districts for the sole purpose of defeating those men. There are enough unregistered poor in each Congressional district to swing any election if they are registered and voted. What Congressman could withstand the prospect of certain defeat? And having defeated those chosen, how would other Congressmen behave in the next Congress not knowing whether they would be chosen for liquidation in the next election?

The New Left has tried to create a sense of revolution in the nation by shouting slogans and marching up and down the streets. But when the hated establishment is left secure in its citadel, certain that it cannot be dislodged, then it has very little reason to pay attention to them and maintains the power to suppress them. The New Left should use the system to create uncertainty in the minds of Congressmen it dislikes so that all would tend to change lest lightning strike them in their next election.

In a comparable manner the executive branch of the government could be easily changed if sufficient pressure were applied to it through proper channels. When we speak of America as a democracy, we often fool ourselves. While we vote for our Senators, Congressmen, and Governors, we do not get a chance to vote for the multitude of civil servants which they are able to appoint. Thus the majority of people in the system are placed there without citizen approval.

This fact should not cause people to give up on the system. Simply because a man is appointed to a position, or through the drudgery of years has followed the Peter Principle and risen to his level of incompetence, does not mean he is immortal. There has never been a system yet that would not gladly sacrifice one of its own for a moment's peace, no matter how brief. If the system is to be changed, then those who would change it should pinpoint its weak spot, its blockage points, and place all the pressure on that one point until the blockage is cleared.

It makes little sense to rail against the ineptness of the Small Business Administration, the Justice Department, or Health, Education and Welfare if the threats and complaints are voiced in generalities. The natural tendency of the system is to gather itself together and attempt to justify its existence. After the report *Hunger U.S.A.* came out, a reply was called for from those people administering the food-stamp programs in the respective states. As could be expected, no hunger, malnutrition, or even gauntness could be found by those people who were administering the program. Yet it was clearly evident that hunger and malnutrition stalked the nation's poor in all areas of the nation.

The follow-up to the *Hunger* report should have been an identification of specific individuals who were not administering the program correctly. The federal and state governments would have been more than happy to sacrifice one man than to continue to bear the heat of sustained public outcry against them. In that way and within a short time the channels for distribution of surplus commodities and food stamps would have been cleared for action. Bureaucrats would have bent over backward to run their programs, living always in the fear that the spotlight would suddenly focus on them.

At the present time churches are rent internally by the fact that their national staffs are doormats to militants, while the local church parishes, dioceses, and presbyteries are forbidden to use church funds for local projects and are supposed to raise funds which the national church headquarters will disburse as it sees fit. Perhaps the local parishes could place all their collections in escrow until the national churches regain their senses; even better, they could use their funds for local projections to assist minority groups and youth in their own locales. In short order they would redirect the misguided programs which their national staffs are advocating and which are splitting the churches.

Every system has certain procedures by which it regulates its internal life. Each system is based upon the mathematical assumption that a certain problem can occur only so often, and therefore only a certain amount of staff is needed to keep the total operation working. Martin Luther King, Jr., used this weakness of the system to great advantage in his demonstrations. Knowing that Southern cities could not possibly jail everyone who marched, he worked carefully to fill up the jails until it became impossible for the system to punish everyone, and the day was won.

In like manner the march of twenty-five thousand people in protest over the brutality of the police during the "People's Park" controversy in Berkeley simply overloaded the ability of the system to respond, and the march had to be allowed to proceed. If the concept of administrative overload were used consistently with selected targets, the system would have to respond to adapt itself to the new conditions. There has never been a concentrated campaign to overload certain systems with paperwork until they change their method of operation or cease to exist.

Campus militancy in like manner could create a legal havoc of undreamed proportions without a harsh word being spoken. Instead of occupying buildings and issuing demands, organized students could radically change the functioning of a university within a few weeks by using the system's procedures against it. One frivolous example is the "religious preference card," which must be filled in during every registration session so that the campus chaplain can follow mama's boy or girl through his or her college career with hayrides and Thanksgiving baskets for the poor and other relevant church activities. Suppose twenty-five thousand students rebelled and listed "Baalist" or "Dagonist" or "Jupiterian" as their religion and these cards all went through the university IBM machines. In short order religious preference cards would become obsolete.

There are an incredible number of tactics which could be used to bring about a radical change in present structures. Use of them depends upon how clearly those people advocating change want a change and understand the nature of the system they are facing. This means strategy by which moral and ethical questions can be raised so that they will convey a maximum of issue-education while making maximal use of the weaknesses of the system. In that way the good things within a system would be made better and a real type of guerrilla warfare, though on a more sophisticated level, could be waged with deadly effectiveness. There would also be no way in which the revolution could devour its creators.

It must be remembered that, in an electric world, systems are virtually helpless against sudden and well conceived movements. But continual hammering on one point, using one type of tactic, soon brings across the message of conflict to society, and society reacts in an oppressive fashion, thinking that by crushing this one attack it can save itself. The present techniques used by the New Left are childish and as insignificant as the old Indian charges at the wagon train—and about as effective. Since Indians have learned new and flexible techniques after being driven off from the wagon train time after time, it would seem that others could learn also.

4 * THE LIBERAL PROBLEM

THE LIBERAL COMMUNITY is suddenly being regarded as the Judas of the contemporary scene. Whereas Bayard Rustin used to speak of the great coalition of conscience, younger people no longer place much faith in this silent majority. Martin Luther King, Jr., said that "over the last few years many Negroes have felt that their most troublesome adversary was not the John Birch Society, but the white liberal who is more devoted to 'order' than to justice, who prefers tranquillity to equality."

Perhaps the chief reason that the white liberal appears in such a demonic role is that he appears at times of crisis and not during times of tranquillity. Liberal concern is directly proportionate to the pleas of the disadvantaged or oppressed. Hence the role of the liberal has been one of participation in events as an invited guest and not as an enduring partner. Liberals have therefore only had to learn the slogans of change and not the philosophical world in which change makes sense.

Stokely Carmichael and Charles Hamilton chastised the churches, saying: "To begin with, many of those religious groups were available only until the bills were passed, their sustained moral force is not on hand for the all-important process of ensuring federal implementation of those laws." This is precisely the role that churches have played, and often they have overplayed that role, because *that is exactly the role they were asked to play.* No deeper level of involvement has been sought by minority groups of churches and liberals. Since minority groups have always accepted the symbols of liberals, all they really needed was a liberal-religious reaffirmation of the validity of the symbols they had been taught—through action in crises.

Immediately prior to the announcement of Black Power, liberals had seized upon the tremendous morality of the civil rights movement to impose their will upon the nation while garnering laurels which self-righteousness bestows upon itself. So committed were white liberals to playing the role they conceived for themselves that they deluded themselves into thinking they had created the civil rights movement. That field had become their own bailiwick and woe unto the man who intruded upon their private playground. President Johnson, for example, after the tragedies of the Selma march, convinced himself and then the majority of Congress, that whites had created the slogan "We Shall Overcome." Indeed, news commentators remarked on how skillfully Johnson had woven the slogan into the speech before Congress and how this had taken the play away from the black leadership. It was not, if you will remember, until Reverend James Reeb, a white man, was killed, that people began getting upset about the situation in Selma. When white liberals get hurt, things happen.

Martin Luther King, Jr., in his last book, sketches out this type of liberal attitude in classic fashion:

> During the Meredith Mississippi March, when some of the young activists were saying, "We don't want white," Bishop Moore of the Episcopal Church said to Walter Fauntroy of the Washington office of SCLC: "I don't care what they say. That march is protesting a moral evil, an evil detrimental to me and every American. I am going down there *whether they want me or not.*" [Emphasis added.]

Nothing, it might be remarked, matches the self-righteousness of an Episcopal Bishop when he feels he is doing something "relevant." Had Bishop Moore caught the first flight to Montgomery when King began his lonely boycott in 1955, one would have been able to accept Moore's pietism as a valid expression of moral outrage. History books have left Bishop Moore's role in the Montgomery bus boycott unrecorded, however. They do record his stubborn refusal to recognize the birth of Black Power during the Meredith March.

Liberals have trodden the path of Bishop Moore for the past decade. When they have become committed to an ideology they have considered it their own private game which bears no relation to the aspirations of the poor, the black, Indian, or Chicano. They have been careful to support only popular movements and have entered the fray only after movements have become popular.

Thus with Black Power the initial reaction of liberals who had been involved with racial minorities was one of surprise and shock. They had done yeoman work in bringing the issue of discrimination to the attention of the lethargic white majority. Suddenly it seemed as if the minority groups were deliberately rejecting the most precious gift the liberals could bestow. I remember various people who, on learning of Red Power, told me they didn't know whether they approved or not! It was not within their thought structure to conceive that we might want to do things ourselves. They were firmly convinced that unless they did it, we would never succeed.

The power movements of the last few years were initially designed to give a maximum flexibility to the masses of people in the racial communities and to allow the problems as seen from within those communities to occupy the center stage. But it was not to be. In typical American fashion, the liberals, who were assumed to be obsolete once power was delivered into the hands of the people, quickly made their peace with the ideology of power, learned the slogans and battle cries, and sallied forth as advocates of power and self-determination.

Having accepted black and related "powers" in 1967 and 1968, liberals embarked on a campaign to "give" self-determination to the powerless. At first they raised large amounts of money, particularly in the churches. The Episcopal Church, for example, had a crisis fund of $9 million for disbursement to the disenfranchised. The United Church of Christ and the Presbyterians had similar amounts for the same type of program. The National Council of Churches created the Inter-religious Foundation for Community Organization, a high-overhead, low-yield conglomerate of divinely commissioned do-gooders.

The crisis funds were administered by newly arrived liberals who flatly stated that racial minorities had not made progress because their leaders had become "establishment types." Consequently, they felt that the only way to disburse the crisis money was to check each applicant to see if he fitted their conception of the frustrated black, Indian, or Mexican who was oppressed by the establishment.

The chief method of distinguishing good guys from bad guys was whether or not they believed in "confrontation." If an Indian swore he believed in "confrontation" and promised to burn the agency building when he got home, he was eligible for funds. If he was uncertain about assassinating the Secretary of the Interior, then he was classified as a "conservative racist" and was not funded. I never was funded because I couldn't endorse the wholesale destruction of the Bureau of Indian Affairs. Mediocrity is not, after all, a moral sin. The result of this attitude was the wholesale liquidation of recognized leadership in the various racial communities in favor of the flamboyant demagogue who could "tell it like it is." Liberals would only talk to people from racial groups who parroted the liberal party line of their terrible suffering from white racism. What was so hilarious was that these supposed "militants" were trying to get white racist money in white racist New York City where they stayed in white racist hotels at thirty white racist dollars a night and ate white racist food. Most of the militants went to white racist nightclubs and drank at white racist bars where they were waited upon by white racist bartenders. (They did drink Carling's *Black* Label beer and *Red* Label Scotch, however.) In effect the liberals compounded the very sins against the racial minorities which Carmichael and Hamilton had outlined as the pattern of classic co-optation. They only talked with people who used the same violence-oriented rhetoric which they had previously learned from post-SNCC black leadership.

Some of the events of the past two years have remained with me as classic examples of liberal nonsense. In December, 1968, the Episcopal Church passed a resolution creating a committee to make a presentation on Indian work. This church has been notorious for its refusal to recruit native clergy in its Indian missions. When the committee was announced, two Indian "radicals" were named as members. The two, who happen to be good friends and occasional allies of mine, are erstwhile leaders of a certain clique in Indian politics. They are not, however, in the classic machine-gun-carrying mold of the more spectacular black leadership, nor are they Episcopalians.

I fought to keep them from the committee because the committee was designed to present the story of the deprivation of Indian people inside the Episcopal Church by Episcopalians. The committee was not designed to fund a frontal attack on the Bureau of Indian Affairs. But the black paternalists and white liberals with the church had a veritable hemorrhage because they insisted that the times required people to "tell it like it is" and that militants should be represented.

Finally, they were taken off, and Hank Adams, militant leader of the Fish-ins of the Northwest, was added to the committee in their place. When we had our first meeting, Hank appeared in sweater and slacks, spoke in a soft, low, intelligent manner and presented many thoughtful insights into the problems of Indian people with the Christian churches.

The liberals of the Episcopal Church were livid. They had expected Hank to roar into the building on his motorcycle, shoot the reception clerk, assault the presiding Bishop for his racist tactics, and spend his waking hours carving up the "white racist" furniture. Their complaint was classic: "Hank Adams doesn't TALK like a militant, HE DOESN'T EVEN DRESS LIKE A MILITANT."

Alack and alas, Hank had forgotten and I had neglected to remind him, that Indian leaders, like other leaders of racial communities, WORE SUNGLASSES. So Hank was read off the rolls of salvation and I was branded as "forked-tongued" because they thought we had misrepresented Hank as a militant when he obviously wasn't militant. (Hank was out on appeal from two convictions of fishing out of season at the time.)

Of such blessed insights into the nature of social change is the liberal religious establishment possessed. It used to be that by their works ye shall know them. Now the saying is, if they ain't got sunglasses, they ain't real. I suspect, but cannot prove, that a secret commission within the Christian establishment is visiting the churches and seminaries and painting in sunglasses on the paintings of the saints to make them seem more religious.

Thus, instead of the past several years having been years in which racial communities consolidated their power and developed programs for human development—as *Black Power* had originally demanded—these have been years of utter nonsense. White liberals have played politics within racial communities and have raised a nonrepresentative dictatorial leadership to replace the existing moderate leadership.

Much contemporary leadership in racial communities is recognized only in liberal circles. These leaders earn their living by attending liberal conferences as performing animals suited only for "telling it like it is." Never have so many done so little for so few and so expensively. But the problem is deeper than that. White liberalism has, under the guise of racial integrity for racial minorities, successfully lifted the ancient "white man's burden" from the souls of white folk. It has become invalid for whites to even venture a guess as to what is happening in racial communities. Whites have thus been left to fend for themselves simply because they are white!

I have never been one to advocate whites doing anything that Indians could do better. But what if one has no Indians at hand to do a job? Does it then remain undone? In today's world it does. The white liberal establishment has not yet reached the point of sophisticated thought where it can conceive of demagoguery within projects and programs which it is funding. It is caught in a logical circle of paranoia in which everything is interpreted according to the mythology of oppression. The way out of oppression, for the white liberal, is to deny that any good can ever come out of a coalition that crosses racial lines. When a white is involved in a task which involves racial minorities, it is paternalism per se. No further thought is given to the problem or the situation.

The upshot of the power movements has been that a fairly substantial number of intelligent whites have been liquidated from the intergroup scene and replaced by liberal do-gooders and their pets. The vast middle ground of nearly inert white sympathizers has had to polarize around the problems of racism and self-determination, in effect creating a much larger number of white racists.

One could not believe the zeal and self-righteousness with which the liquidation has taken place in racial communities unless one had been an active participant during the last several years. One Episcopal report recommending the funding of Charles Evers' political rivals in the black community in Mississippi stated that Charles Evers was the biggest "Uncle Tom" in the state. Charles Evers? CHARLES EVERS? Yup. This was the ex cathedra pronouncement after an evening "evaluation" of the state of Mississippi by the Episcopal Church. When quizzed about how an evaluator could reach such stupendous conclusions in less than a day, the people administering the funds replied, "when you know what you're doing you can."

The last few years have a parallel only in the Spanish Inquisition, where a person once declared a heretic had to confess immediately and be put to death or else he was tortured to death in an effort to gain a confession. It has reminded me of the statement that the members of the House of David live forever—of course now and then a nonbeliever within the group is discovered—when he dies.

Unfortunately for the liberals, their preemption of existing leadership has not only blurred the issues by which racial communities were able to distinguish them from the real racists, it has built up a tremendous resentment among minority group leadership against white intruders of any stripe. In attempting to overcome racism through overturning existing leadership in racial communities, liberals have tremendously lessened the possibility of creating a moderate coalition in the future between their forces and actual recognized leaders of racial minorities.

What is so doubly tragic about the liberal intrusion into the politics of the respective racial groups is the fact that Black Power projects a series of strong and valid coalitions when racial communities have gathered power unto themselves. Carmichael and Hamilton said that "All parties to the coalition must perceive a mutually beneficial goal based on the conception of each party of his own self-interest." By playing the political game with racial minorities, liberals have created the self-interest of leadership protecting itself from the intrusions of liberally funded rivals. Coalitions, at the present time, are conspiracies in which one must guard his back more than he must beware of what faces him.

Not only has the cross-racial coalition been handicapped as a vehicle for expression of liberal views, but young whites have themselves left the liberal camp in increasing numbers. Many young whites have found themselves preempted and rendered defenseless in the drive of traditional liberalism to maintain itself. And young whites have rebelled in more spectacular fashion than have minority groups. The manifestations of this movement are everywhere. The plaintive bleating of S. I. Hayakawa during the San Francisco State crisis that the radicals were after the liberals is a sign of this rejection. The confrontation by youth of the traditional liberal Democratic establishment in Chicago during the convention is such a sign. The systematic disruption of the colleges and universities is another smoke signal that even white youth are getting tired of being pushed aside by irrelevant and pious liberals spouting rhetoric which they obviously do not believe.

That is not to say that liberalism has become impotent. Liberals still control the white power structure. In many cases they control it more firmly than they did at the beginning of the civil rights movement. Liberals have firmly entrenched themselves in churches, government agencies, and private organizations. The struggle of the future will be against liberal preemption of the ideas, programs, and beliefs of the underground, into liberal elements which will consist of people of all age groups and racial and ethnic backgrounds who want to get something done.

Liberalism has lost its credibility. It no longer catches up the spirit of the times. Where the conservative is reactionary the liberal is reactive. The liberal waits for movements to occur and then either casually, self-righteously, and unconsciously buys them up or frantically tries to relate to them. The conservative views everything with suspicion. To him even the subway is subversive because it is, after all, an underground movement. The liberal waits to find out if someone else thinks the subway is good or bad, and then pounces on the most popular viewpoint, accepting it as his own and lashing out self-righteously at those who disagree with him.

Indians should be ecstatic that the days of the liberal are waning. No other group has suffered as much at the hands of liberals as have Indians. Where whites "believe" in equality and are active in civil rights when they relate to the black community, they have been "interested" in Indians. It is rather like the way I am interested in collecting coins or someone else is interested in postage stamps. The liberal interest, unfortunately, is a vested interest.

At least among Indians, and I would suspect among other groups as well, it was the liberal who first started "keeping score." In the past, whenever an Indian did something significant, like support some white liberal's program for Indians, the liberal stated that the Indian was a "credit to his race." This accolade was almost comparable to being named chief—and everyone knows how dear that is to the Indian soul.

For the past generation Indians have scrambled over each other trying to become a "credit to their race." I was never much interested in that. We already had one continent, seventy-five million buffalo, half a million dead, the loss of most of a way of life and other credits to our race. I always believed that it was time for us to cash in our credit and live on it.

As the influence of liberals has declined, the significance of many events has also lessened. When poverty was discovered, the "do-good" element jumped into the fray with the enthusiasm of Prince Valiant swinging his "singing sword." Flying to and fro from conference to conference, the liberals filled the world with the sound of airplanes, where it was formerly occupied with music. Now rumor has it that United Airlines may have to mothball half its fleet as the desperate urge to confer begins to ebb.

The primary use of the conference was to provide an "impartial forum" where the great debates of the issues of our time could be conducted. In reality, the liberal used the conference format to inform himself of what was happening so that he would appear relevant. The same vocabulary, the same code words, the same philosophical frame of reference highlighted conferences so that social movements became self-contained and if anything was brought to a conference where liberals gathered that was new, people could not recognize it.

Times have indeed changed. The liberal thought-world has vanished mysteriously along with the concepts which made it valid. Basic philosophical considerations have more and more become necessary. It is no longer valid to consider social problems in isolation or to promote single-answer solutions to long-standing social dilemmas. Since Marshall McLuhan's devastating critique of communications and his delineation of its impact on the world, racial minorities have been forced to take another look at their problems. Liberal preemption of issues and technical vocabulary are now proving useful because they force meaningful transmission of values and issues to seek new words and thought patterns.

Racial groups have been indiscriminately lumped together by the liberal establishment and solutions have been sought which would encompass all groups. Poverty itself has become a general term in which racial minorities are categorized per se without an examination of how and to whom poverty occurs among the respective groups.

It has become traditional to cry over the plight of Indian people. Yet a people with fifty-four million acres of land worth $3 billion should not be in a state of poverty, nor should they have a "plight." Liberals have tended to equate the Southern red-necked sheriff and the Bureau of Indian Affairs. Thus we have had people ask us how we got off the reservation, how often we are beaten by government agents, and how they can help us to become free. They continue to talk about "organizing" the poor Indians as if we were some conglomerate slum population that was dependent upon their goodwill for survival, in spite of the fact that Indian tribes have been organized as federally chartered corporations under the Indian Reorganization Act of 1934 for over a generation.

Because the liberal always took it upon himself to speak for and about the various racial minorities, issues which affected all racial groups were always interpreted to each group as if they shared a common burden. In fact they did share a common burden—the liberal. His style and language have served to divide people rather than to bring them together. No matter how much he hoped to mass all racial groups into the same bag, people in the respective communities knew that they were not receiving the true facts.

The political exiles of the past several years have had a chance to meditate on the strengths and shortcomings of their groups and of themselves. People now understand the necessity of clarifying issues along philosophical lines rather than continuing to spout meaningless rhetoric simply because it is popular among the liberal friends with whom they are confronted.

Traditionally, the problems of racial minorities have been grouped around two poles: the individual and the group. When Indians and Mexicans demand the right to develop their group strengths, liberals rush in to confuse the issue with meaningless questions about the salvation of the individual. When we tried to get a revolving loan fund for tribes, liberals would ask: "But how does this do anything for the individual Indian?" If the blacks demanded the integration of the individual, they were told that getting a few blacks educated would not solve the problems of the black race.

Group salvation has certain philosophical overtones which cannot be denied. In the scheme of individual salvation, time is of the essence. One has only one lifetime to harvest the goodies of the world. It is therefore imperative that one use the most direct methods to amass wealth, prestige, and power. With a group-tribalistic approach to life, time is meaningless. If we do not accomplish the task in our lifetimes, someone else will do so in their time. Strategy can now be projected for a generation or more, whereas the civil rights movement, a product of the liberal world, lived from crisis to crisis, feeding on urgency.

Individual salvation creates a certain amount of impatience. One cannot be bought off with promises. One cannot run away to fight another day. One must have a solution during one's lifetime. These days and the philosophy which they projected are gone forever. Things now have urgency to the degree that they are within the logical scheme of development. The potential for violence is thus much greater in certain events than it is in others.

Demands take on a much more non-negotiable aspect than they did formerly.

Liberalism took the ideals and dreams of Western European civilization and dangled them in front of the blacks and young while attempting to force them on the Mexicans and Indians. Then liberalism couldn't produce. The ideals of the Constitution proved unable to hurdle such roadblocks as Congressional seniority, vested economic interests, the impotent morality of a Christian religion that was "of the world but not in it." Liberalism pushed the ideology of Western man to its logical extremes and it was found to be unsuitable for racial minorities. It also failed the times and the youth who created the times.

The new world, the world in which blacks, Mexicans, Indians, youth, and disenfranchised whites of all ages live, is non-Western in conceptualization and philosophy. It seeks to rule technology and not to be ruled by it. It uses the communications media to its own advantage while people of the old world cringe in terror at the impact of communications. People are fast losing their emotional commitment to the value system of the Anglo-Saxon tradition. Western European concepts no longer rule men's minds, they have been demythologized.

In the next decade we shall see constant turmoil between the adherents of the old world and the pioneers of the new world. Richard Nixon is a fitting symbol of the old world and it is perhaps proper that he preside over the major part of the change. The new Nixon is a man of commercially created image. He has already slain his pink ladies in his effort to reach the top. He cannot afford to tarnish the new image by slaying any more. So he has little choice but to mediate between two antithetical forces which he neither understands nor trusts.

With the negation of traditional Western values the chances of a revival of Indians and Mexicans through nationalistic movements have considerably increased. Being non-Western and instinctively oriented toward group values, they can now bring their special genius to bear on their problems. But they must hurry. With militant young blacks and disenchanted white youth rapidly forming combinations on the tribal-clan basis, Indians and Mexicans may well miss the nationalistic boat. They run the risk of being the last middle-class people in the United States.

One example should suffice. In the last several years we have seen a tremendous surge in popularity in the concept of bilingual education. Indians and Mexicans have swallowed this concept as though it were manna from heaven. For too many of them, bilingual education is an affirmation of the validity of their language. But it is not that at all. Bilingual education is designed primarily to assist them to learn English so that they can better assimilate into the conglomerate of suburban nothingness.

Instead of swallowing the poisons of bilingual education meekly, Mexicans and Indians should raise the question of the validity of their languages in and of themselves. They should seek to become expertly fluent in both languages and insist that schools teach whites their languages.

The Kerner Report eloquently testifies to this liberal conception of the world. It was designed, admittedly, to identify the causes of ghetto uprisings. It naïvely assumes, however, that blacks have been a part of the development of the nation until the present and it naïvely advances this premise: "One nation is moving toward two societies, one black, one white—separate and unequal."

The Kerner Report assumes that FORMERLY this country was one, that RECENTLY it is moving toward two unequal societies. As concerns black and white, this nation has not yet been one, and if it has been one it has been a white one.

What the Kerner Report should have said, had it had insight into the nature of American society and understood the white world view, is that among people who have previously held to a white world view, society is splitting between black and white. The Kerner Report should have restricted itself to a commentary on the dissolution of the white thought structure, the split between value systems of white and black. Indians and Mexicans have never been a part of that world of which the Kerner Report speaks. There was never a time in which these two groups did not fight the white thought patterns into which they were being forced.

The Kerner Report further concluded that "to pursue our present course will involve the continuing polarization of the American community and, ultimately, the destruction of basic democratic values." When did the United States ever have basic democratic values? Taking democracy at its lowest common denominator, one man one vote, what democratic values are to be destroyed in Alabama, Louisiana, Mississippi, and Georgia, where blacks are systematically prevented from voting? This is precisely the problem with the Kerner Report. It warns us about white racism, which is not a new discovery, but it does not really examine the possible alternative ideologies which should be considered if we are even to solve the problem of white racism.

The ultimate tragedy is that the masses in each community, white and the respective minority groups, appear to understand each other far better than do the leaders of the groups. People continue to ask me to whom Indians say "leave us alone." In most cases Indian people are not talking about their white acquaintances, who have been helpful in the past on an individual basis. Many of these people have offered specific technical skills, have raised funds for us, sponsored events so that we can present our message, and done yeoman volunteer work on behalf of the various Indian causes. We will need that type of assistance for some time to come.

The liberals who create havoc within the minority groups are people in the official structure, be it church or state, private or public organization, who wield tremendous amounts of power and who do not for a moment listen to anyone—white, red, black, or Chicano. These are whites and blacks who beat people of goodwill into the ground by calling them do-gooders. This tactic raises serious questions in the minds of many whites as to their ability to help minority groups. By blasting the motives of the average man, the liberals within the power structure are able to raise themselves as knowledgeable authority figures to whom the common citizen then cedes all power and funding sources, asking only that the problem be resolved.

It is time that the man in the pew, the taxpayer, the contributor, cleaned house. A great many people inhabiting American organizations and government agencies pay no attention to either the supporters or the subjects of programs. They are concerned primarily with their own survival and continuance of power. We desperately need the development of responsible "white power" to invade the churches, foundations, government agencies, and welfare organizations and restore a semblance of sanity to them. People in minority groups badly need assistance in many areas. They are not receiving it because they are expected to hew to preestablished ideologies that exist primarily in the minds of powerful liberal administrators. Until we can get intelligent and responsible whites to speak up in their own communities there is not much we can do to solve our own problems or to reduce the tensions that exist between groups; tensions that at present are caused by unwitting misinterpretation of liberal understandings of the world.

5 * OTHERS

Sometimes, when people ask me what tribe I belong to, I am tempted to answer "Others." There is really a valid reason to consider oneself an "other" if one is an Indian. I have yet to attend a conference on poverty, race relations, social problems, civil rights, or pollution without being tagged an "other." A quick survey of other Indian people has revealed that they also consider themselves "others." Anthropologists, who receive the word from on high every evening when the rest of us are watching television, speak reverently of this phenomenon as "Pan-Indianism." Pan-Indianism is a label used to paste over the efforts of Indian tribes to organize for effective political action. Knowing anthropologists and sociologists sneer at efforts to organize as "merely pan-Indianism," thinking that by labeling it they have understood and disarmed it.

But being an "other" has much more serious consequences when policies are decided and programs developed. Massive conferences are held where important speakers articulate the most fantastic ideology of modern society. When it comes time for questions and the audience begins to disperse for greener fields, Indian people occasionally ask what the effect of the proposal would be for them. The answer is that this program is for whites, blacks, labor, migrants, Mexicans, Appalachian folk, and OTHERS. Presidents making their stirring State of the Union speeches each January outline the domestic programs of their administrations in such ringing and definite terms that one is tempted to cross the Red Sea ahead of the rest of the nation. But Indians listening hard for a word from the wise find that the programs are for whites, blacks, labor, migrants, Mexicans, Appalachian folk, the "silent majority," the "effete intellectuals," the "Communist menace," and OTHERS.

One could conclude that there are not really any Indians in American society, but that it has been infiltrated by OTHERS. In fact when Indians and blacks first began to talk to each other, Indians always thought that blacks were addressing them as OTHERS until they discovered that the blacks were using another word quite similar in sound but having another meaning.

It would not be so bad being an other if the word meant something; generally, it does not. It is just a polite way of including you in something that you later find you really didn't want to be included in. By the time you find out that being an other has no advantages, you are already trapped in a meaningless cycle of policies that merely repeat your otherness to you in an infinite variety of ways. The foremost arena in which this occurs is in the vague field known as race relations. When I was on the Executive Council of the Episcopal Church, they had a committee to study racism in society. (They dared not look for it inside the church where it abounded.) A well-known clergyman was presenting his conclusions, and he spoke exclusively about the black problem. When I questioned him about the report and its importance to Indian people, he told me that the study would be expanded to include Mexicans, migrants, in fact all of God's (and the white man's) children, AND INDIANS TOO.

The point that I was trying to make, which unfortunately no one understood, was that race relations has come to be defined exclusively in terms of the the white-black relationship. Whenever other groups are mentioned, the speaker instantly says, "and others too" as if by merely mentioning other groups he was including them in his frame of reference. Having defined a specific problem —white-black—people feel they can forever include additional groups without losing the meaning of the words they are using, and it just ain't so.

Using a vocabulary that has definite meaning for whites and blacks does not remotely relate to other groups. Thus equality in a white-black context means that the black man should have equal legal rights and economic opportunities in his individual capacity as white citizens. In a Mexican-Anglo context the word equality may very well take on the sense that somewhere along the line Mexicans have been deprived of their rights to specific pieces of land guaranteed to them by treaties with Mexico. In an Indian-white context this specifically means the surrender by the white of his eternal quest for the key to turn an Indian into a Western European immigrant.

The whole field of relationships between the different groups in society has been perverted by failing to understand the necessity to change words and meanings when dealing with different groups. Thus "intergroup relations" has become synonymous with race relations, which means whites and blacks. There has NEVER been an understanding of how groups relate to each other. It has always been a case of comparing imagined goals of the black community in its struggle to become like whites with whatever is said by Indians and Mexicans, and recently by youth, so that everything comes out even. But it never does.

To assure a proper understanding of intergroup relations we must talk about the real relationships between the respective groups that compose American society. Intergroup relations is thus an extremely complex field in which all groups are related to each other according to their experiences of each other, exclusive of their relationships with other groups. There is an Indian-black relationship and an Indian-white relationship that remains hidden and unexamined if one is simply to lump Indians into the white-black vocabulary and thought-world by saying AND INDIANS TOO.

The whole of American society has been brainwashed into believing that if it understood blacks it could automatically understand every other group simply because blacks were the most prominent minority group with which white society had to deal. Many whites are therefore stunned when they discover the current Indian slogan of "leave us alone." In the white-black terminology this is a threatening phrase because it implies that no contact should occur between races. Blacks have not had to suffer the stifling paternalism that Indians have suffered from churches, universities, and state and federal governments. Blacks have been able to develop their own version of religion, including liturgy and congregational participation, that answers their needs. Indians have been systematically denied this right.

While blacks have had to fight for legal rights to develop their own institutions, Indians have had a multitude of institutions that were ostensibly theirs, yet they have been deprived of the right to operate them in the way that the in people saw fit. Blacks have had the advantage of alliances with elements of white society on a nearly equal basis. During the civil rights struggle young whites came South and worked with black people because they believed in the fight for equal rights and because they felt that integration was God's will. But whites coming to Indian country came primarily to "experience" Indians. I spoke at a conference of educators one year and described the reservations and how we needed specific help in educational projects. After the talk a woman came gushing up to me and said that she was so interested in having a work camp go out to Indian country because she wanted her children to have THAT EXPERIENCE.

Now I could think of a lot of exotic experiences that Indians could provide for wandering college students with a summer to kill. But it is damn depressing to realize that your tribe exists at the sufferance of a society because it can be experienced. Because Indians are always categorized as others, whites have no reason to expect anything else, since they are regarded as merely another species of minority-group Americanus. Being merely an experience with nothing more to contribute than a few exciting pages in a diary creates an incredible gap between Indian people and others that cannot be bridged easily.

The Kerner Report seriously announces that society is splitting into two separate and unequal societies. This report is premised on the idea that at one time society was a monolith of opportunity and brotherhood. It overlooks the fact that blacks and whites have never shared one society. But more important, it overlooks the fact that tribalistic people and individualistic people have never shared anything in common. American society has always been divided into the mainstream white and black Americans who shared integrationist philosophies and the Indians, Mexicans, Jews, and ethnic concentrations who stubbornly held traditions and customs brought over from the old country. These are the OTHERS so casually mentioned when social problems are discussed.

Race relations basically means the relationship between blacks and whites. It is built upon the old slave-master tradition by which the races have been separated through history. It is fundamentally an economic concept that finds its most eloquent expression and most of its problems in the ownership and use of property. The struggle in education has not been over what KIND of education should be given but over the OPPORTUNITY and EQUALITY of the education received. Assuming that the education crisis could have been solved in the year following the Supreme Court decision outlawing segregation, the natural development would have been the total integration of black children into white schools and the abolishment of dual school systems based upon race.

Looking at race relations on the basis of groups would have been an entirely different matter. Schools would have been under fire for the content of their courses rather than equality in filling classroom seats. The struggle would have been between the aforementioned groups over the view of the world, the orientation of history courses, the language requirements, and the definition of curriculum. This is the important thing that society must recognize today. The constant warfare between students of minority groups and college and university administrators over ethnic studies courses indicates that the definitions that formerly held society in a white-black tension over equality of opportunity have vanished. In their place has come the demand to revise courses to conform to the conceptions each group has of itself.

Present vocabulary in the field of race relations cannot explain this movement in the colleges. Nor can American society really understand the fight over religious education. In recent years the courts have been flooded with suits concerning the separation between church and state, and the issue of government funds going into church schools has created a furor. This movement has been complemented by concern over the banning of prayers in schools. Again we are seeing a redefinition of social issues according to the values of specific groups. In the case of religious controversy it could be said that there are different "races" of religion fighting for supremacy or at least for equality of opportunity to define themselves.

Putting aside obvious racial prejudice, the battle over neighborhood schools can also be considered in a new light. People are becoming vitally concerned about their children being bussed miles across large cities because they are finally becoming aware of the need for neighborhood. The sense of community is rising and yet it is constantly being used as a thinly disguised stalking horse on the racial issue. There is, however, a real concern that once the neighborhoods are broken up, alienation will be complete, since the schools stand as the last hope of white America that some kind of community can be preserved.

A significant number of important social issues have been misunderstood because they have been swept under the table by superficial handling of the problems that affect people. There have been too many OTHERS in every phase of social existence. American society has not really examined its problems on a meaningful level of thinking. Instead, the racial issue has swept every issue into a white-black polarization that defines everything according to its traditional concepts.

We are now watching the dissolution of the very concept of white as the ethnic groups assert their respective identities. Tensions are becoming unbearable because programs, laws, governments, and communications media have been oriented exclusively toward outworn words and narrow ideas. Yet these very institutions and media are having a tribalizing effect that pulls elements of society farther apart. While the world appears to be shattering, it is in many respects opening the frozen world of white-black relationships and including OTHERS. To be more specific society has traditionally polarized between black and white, and both poles are differentiating themselves into component groups, thus invalidating the very ideas and concepts that created the polarization.

The dissolution of polarity itself would be excellent except that the economic system and more importantly the distribution system used by capitalist economics is massed behind the polarization. Society is thus virtually helpless when it comes to solving social and economic problems because it has arranged its means of solving problems in a manner in which interests are vested according to old concepts. The poor cannot be fed with surplus foods because the government is set up to buy whatever surpluses the farmers produce, and anything that they overproduce becomes surplus. Joseph Heller was centered on American society when he wrote *Catch-22*, for contemporary society is a complicated matrix of *Catch-22*—one that unfortunately holds itself together tighter than the best adhesive.

Housing becomes an OTHERS when superhighways are discussed. Pollution becomes an OTHERS when industrial development is discussed. Land becomes an OTHERS when new suburbs are planned or when a jetport is needed. Religion is an OTHERS when wars are planned and war becomes an OTHERS when church services are held. Another way of describing this process is that American society has so functionalized itself that it is unable to function as a society. Things are used and not experienced and it is at this point that the Indian experience and tribalism becomes quite important, because Indians are always experienced!!

Whites can logically work for a principle that exists because of the white-black relationship. Integration and separatism become live options for both whites and blacks because they are merely alternative options to the polarization. Funds can be raised to either support or fight, for both explain the world in simplistic terms that can claim one's mind and dominate the processes by which men think. But when a people can only be experienced it is very hard to raise funds for them. They are always using the funds for FOREIGN purposes. A person cannot work side by side with an experience because he is always swallowed by it. I have known many ex-VISTAS who could not forget their days on the reservations for years afterward. They continued to write articles describing their arrival at certain reservations. They made recorded detailed observations on everything that happened to them while they were with certain tribes.

It would seem to me that the most urgent task of white and black America is to break the endless sparring. They should instead begin to include other groups—specifically Indians—in all their discussions and deliberations. There is a real need for expanded conceptions of the nature of man and society. Renewal cannot come through repetition of old phrases and continual investigations of the white-black relationship. But again this cannot come about because of the tendency to equate their experience of OTHERS with their own familiar relationship.

When Black Power was first dominating discussions, many of us tried to speak meaningfully to blacks about Indian tribalism. Everything we said was passed off as a clumsy attempt to catch on to the coattails of the power movement and ride them to glory. No one would listen to OTHER ideas, such as the need for capital, the idea of the sovereignty of the group, and the necessity for grounding the movement in a land base peculiar to the local community group. When the Forman Manifesto arrived, whites cooed with satisfaction at the thought that they had discovered a new term to describe the white-black relationship. Reparations became the name of the game. Yet behind the Forman Manifesto was the demand for a land base, capital funds for community self-determination, and a recognition of the black caucus as a distinct group in every institution.

Merely bringing Indians into the discussion is no answer at all. It will probably be done in the same contemptuous manner in which Indians and youth—both children in American mythology—have traditionally been treated. Adults, blacks, whites, and bureaucrats contemptuously announce that "we haven't heard from the Indian youth yet." Then a half hour is devoted to listening to their childish prattle which apparently leads nowhere. Finally the adults-whites-blacks get back to the important business for which the conference has been called. The concepts of traditional white-black relationships are so strongly ingrained in people within the bureaucratic structure that it is impossible for them to allow such a new ideological coalition to form.

The result of continuing to view the world through traditional black-white glasses is more rapid escalation of tensions within the social structure. Governments on the municipal and state level simply cannot solve their problems when the polarization is sitting at their doorstep. Consequently, crises in urban areas bring home to people the necessity of developing new social forms for self-preservation. The blackout, heavy snows, garbage and transportation strikes, and rising crime rates have forced people together for survival. Block organizations have been formed in some cities to provide a semblance of order at the neighborhood level. The impact of democratic forms caused by a hostile environment is to tribalize urban people nearly as fast as the communications media.

Even residential patterns are shifting away from an economic determinism. In New York City the trend is still running strong for cooperative housing, while in the rest of the nation condominiums are the fad. The difference is striking and important. In cooperatives, people purchase a share of the building in which their apartment is located. They thus hold the property in common and are able to determine their membership in the enterprise and include or exclude at will according to their own criteria. In condominiums, people purchase specific apartments in a building and there is no regard for other owners as long as services are provided to apartment owners. Condominium apartments can be financed independently of the ownership of the building, while cooperatives simply give a share in the total assets.

The parallel to Indian tribalism is important. Indians hold their lands and assets in common and membership in the tribe is equivalent to membership in the cooperative. Yet Congress has always tried to break up the Indian tribal estate, claiming that holding property in common is the major reason why Indian people fail to make "progress" according to some vaguely defined Congressional standard. The trend to cooperatives belies the traditional language that is used to define society. Cooperatives are an OTHER when housing programs are discussed, so many people miss the fact that they show every indication of becoming the major form of urban housing in the future.

There is no easy answer to changing the outlook of American society to include OTHERS. The very structures by which society is organized have become encrusted with ancient ideas advocated by administrators whose chief claim to fame is their survival within the bureaucracy. In both private and public agencies and organizations the Peter Principle operates with unerring efficiency, creating the minimum impact from the maximum effort.

The present structure is the exact reverse of tribal forms, and consequently power and decision-making flows in reverse channels to the needs of the people. The Civil Service, Congress, and universities and churches reward longevity and seniority and base this process on the supposed wisdom and experience of the career bureaucrat. New people coming into the system begin at the bottom and have to fight their way up the pyramid with their new ideas. By the time they achieve a status level at which they can place some of their ideas into operation, the ideas and people are stagnant and in many cases demoralized and disheartened.

Congressional committees are headed by the oldest members of Congress, some so decrepit and ancient that their staffs have to make all of the decisions, since a responsibility to think would in many cases short-circuit the brain of an old Senator or Congressman who should have retired gracefully years before. In the churches, only the oldest and most pietistic organization men are raised to important posts. Bishops are notoriously out of touch with the modern world and with their own constituency. A symptom of this is the Roman Catholic church's recognition of Galileo's theories in the 1800s—nearly four centuries after the fact. The contemporary struggle over birth control will probably not be resolved until the world is stacked four deep with people.

Indian tribes operate on an entirely different basis. Indian leadership is generally a whole generation younger than the tribal council it must lead. Thus the tribe has the benefit of new ideas and energetic leadership that is tempered by experienced members of the tribe. The average council has a chairman who is thirty to forty years old, with a substantial number of members in their late sixties and seventies. Youth thus has the opportunity to develop ideas that speak to the contemporary world, but official actions of the tribe are oriented toward the collective experiences of the older people. The tribe maintains this tension and is able to meet novel situations and survive their impact.

If the present system were reversed, the OTHERS would soon take charge. The newest members of Congress would become committee chairmen and influence would depend upon the individual member's inexperience in Congress. Older men would be relegated to the lowest posts in the official hierarchy. Yet the young committee chairmen would be subject to the braking actions of the older members, among whom they would have to achieve a consensus in order to develop new programs. In the churches newly ordained men with the vigor of youth would be placed in the highest posts, subject to the necessity of creating a constituency from older, more experienced people to support their programs.

In American politics we have seen this situation occur twice, once with John Kennedy and once with Eugene McCarthy. John Kennedy boldly seized the nomination of the Democratic Party in 1960. He was filled with new ideas and had the vigor of youth in promoting his ideas, but he was subject to the conservative ideas of the older members of Congress and his party. The two forces balanced each other enough so that society began to move as younger people accepted Kennedy's ideas which had been OTHERS, rejected until that time by the older generation. Momentum was built up so that Lyndon Johnson, a master politician, could push through an amazing social program when he became President.

I have never been a John Kennedy fan because I never felt that he kept his promises to Indian people. But I would never deny that he brought new ideas and movement into American society and laid the way for Eugene McCarthy's rise in political life. Younger people had been able to penetrate the layers of bureaucracy with their ideas during the Kennedy years, so that when the Vietnam issue heated up they were able to use McCarthy as their spokesman. The older generation credited McCarthy with the fantastic ability to mobilize youth for political action. Their enthusiasm in raising the war issue carried McCarthy far beyond normal expectations.

Young people are now revolutionizing American politics. They are seizing issues one after another, using older statesmen as their stalking horses to force society to think out the problem. Gaylord Nelson may well become their vehicle for expression of concern about pollution and George McGovern may be forced to represent the concern of youth over hunger and malnutrition. Senators and Congressmen are now subject to the whims of the younger populace and can no longer, in many cases, simply sit back and exercise power according to their own sense of values. The shift of antiwar youth from demonstrations to political action may well be the saving movement of contemporary society.

The university scene is now on the verge of experiencing this shift from domination by older men with stagnant ideas to controlling youthful innovators. Ethnic studies programs and "Free Universities" are crucially important in this change. If the Free Universities can be maintained outside the institutionalized "marketplace of ideas," they will soon be able to produce more thoughtful and creative people than are produced in traditional educational programs. Universities and colleges will be forced to compete with store-front courses in order to keep their students. The net result of this movement will be that education will come to be dominated by creative younger people whose ideas will be tempered by the experience of older people. Administrators will be forced to develop a following among students, instead of the prostitutional fawning in front of the Board of Regents which characterizes education today.

Obviously the most important thing that people can do today in the field of race relations is to develop additional understanding of groups that used to compose the categories of OTHERS. On the one hand, this means that the OTHERS will have to develop political power within the structure and defend the new intellectual territory they are able to forge out. On the other hand, it means that the entire vocabulary and organizational hierarchy must be dissolved in favor of new organizations at the local level. New languages with specific technical content should be developed by local groups to fit their needs. Bureaucrats must either understand the new vocabulary or perish.

The important thing is that intergroup relations take on a real sense of coalition between groups. Whites and blacks must reexamine their conceptions of the world in terms of their relationship with other groups. In many instances this will mean deemphasizing ideas and concepts that the two groups feel are important to themselves. It is a real question of whether or not the militants in the black community and the paramilitary units in the white community will allow this to happen. They may very well push both groups to ultimate confrontation in guerilla warfare incidents. But this again would push the inert silent majority toward neighborhood tribalizing efforts for self-preservation. In short, there are really no alternatives to decentralization, democratization, and tribalization.

6 * ANOTHER LOOK AT BLACK POWER

STOKELY CARMICHAEL'S cry of "Black Power" closed the era of the integrationist-individualist approach to racial problems and ushered in the era of the group as a group. Black Power spoke not only to blacks but also to a longing within the other racial minorities to express the dignity and sovereignty of their own communities. Racial minorities in the United States had suffered under the integrationist concept because they were considered mere conglomerates of individuals, each person being handicapped by his peculiar color, language, and culture. The concept of power, however, meant that the group could speak and demand as a group. Soon every minority community in the nation formed its own power organization. Thus we have had Black Power, Chicano Power, Red Power, Flower Power, and Green Power. One rumor was that the owners of high-rise apartments were forming "Tower Power" to influence rent controls in the large cities.

However, Stokely Carmichael and Charles Hamilton's *Black Power,* which articulated the concept of power for the minority groups, never received the careful and impartial reading it deserved. Their theory of power has been wrongly condemned as the spark which set off the racial fire we now find destroying our country. If we can understand and accept the analysis of intergroup relations contained in *Black Power,* we may yet find a way beyond the violence and hatred that has characterized the last few years.

Primary to *Black Power's* message is the description of the process of co-optation of leadership. The process is common to the experiences of all minority groups, particularly the Indian and Mexican communities:

> In the United States, as in Africa, their [the black leadership] adaptation operated to deprive the black community of its potential skills and brain power. All too frequently these "integrated" people are used to blunt the true feelings and goals of the black masses. They are picked as "Negro" leaders and the white power structure proceeds to talk to and deal only with them. Needless to say, no fruitful, meaningful dialogue can take place under such circumstances. Those handpicked "leaders" have no viable constituency for which they can speak and act. All this is a classic formula of colonial co-optation.

For generations, capable people in the Indian, Mexican, and black communities have been systematically pulled from their communities and set up as "leaders." Their only function as leaders, however, was to affirm the beliefs which white society held about their group. Often they were designated as a "credit to their race," and whites contended that because of the examples set by these leaders the racial minority groups could be salvaged.

But the co-opted leadership could not create a constituency within their own groups. It could only play the role of a cultural Judas-goat. Thus there was no communication between the masses in the minority communities and in white society. The Kerner

Report spotted this gulf but failed to understand the process that had created it. The divisiveness of society was illuminated; it was not a new discovery.

Beyond co-optation, according to Carmichael and Hamilton, lay the need to redefine the black community. The need to "reclaim our history and our identity from what must be called cultural terrorism, from the depredation of self-justifying white guilt" was considered crucial to the development of power by the black community. Martin Luther King, Jr., spoke of this need in his last book: "it is in the context of the slave tradition that some of the ideologies of the Black Power movement call for the need to develop new and indigenous codes of justice for the ghettos, so that blacks may move entirely away from their former masters' 'standards of good conduct.'" Carmichael and Hamilton found their way beyond co-optation by examining the historical experiences of the black community and by creating a contemporary identity which absorbed the historical experience. Black Power became a "call for black people in this country to unite, to recognize their heritage, to build a sense of community." It was a call "for black people to begin to define their own goals, to lead their own organizations and to support those organizations." Black Power was a philosophical activism. Its primary purpose as envisioned by Carmichael and Hamilton was to build local communities into cohesive groups with internal integrity.

But as a philosophically relevant movement, a new vocabulary of technical words outlining a new mythology was essential. "White society devised the language, adopted the rules and had the black community narcotized into believing that that language and those words were, in fact, relevant," they wrote. Negro was replaced by black, short haircuts were grown out into "Afros," and power replaced integration as the rallying cry. In casting aside traditional language and customs, devised by whites, the black community would be faced with the need to acknowledge themselves as a distinct and unique people. "Black people," *Black Power* noted, "have not suffered as individuals but as members of a group; therefore their liberation lies in group action." This idea was the first break from the traditional "integrate-the-individual" doctrine which had dominated the field of intergroup relations for a generation.

Once blacks accepted the validity of their group and resolved the problem of co-optation, they had but one programmatic avenue left to them. "If this [black power] means the creation of parallel community institutions, then that must be the solution," Carmichael and Hamilton concluded. Such a development would leave the door open to the charge of separatism; but separatism was not the conclusion which Carmichael and Hamilton reached. "It is hoped," they said, "that eventually there will be a coalition of poor blacks and poor whites. This is the only coalition which seems acceptable to us, and we see such a coalition as the major internal instrument of change in American society." *Black Power* had indications of reaching a much higher conception of the nature and meaning of a new coalition, but the idea was never fully articulated. "All parties to the coalition," they stated, "must perceive a mutually beneficial goal based on the conception of each party of his own self-interest." One could conclude that the coalition proposed in *Black Power* was essentially an open-ended affair, but it was not.

Carmichael and Hamilton had indicated that a coalition of poor whites and blacks could bring significant internal change in American society. For these poor people, the point of mutual self-interest was poverty, and the context was economics. The first mass attempt to try the coalition was the Poor People's Campaign. But this campaign painfully illustrated that Carmichael and Hamilton had fallen short of a full articulation of the philosophy of the group. Even with the help of Ralph Abernathy, who surpassed the vision of *Black Power* by attracting not only whites and blacks, but Indians and Mexicans as well to the poverty march, the Poor People's Campaign was a disaster.

Once in the nation's capital, bickering broke out among the respective groups. There had been no effort to understand the nature of representation, and only those people willing to raise the issue as individuals participated. When they were confronted with the necessity of speaking for their communities, each group discovered that it had to undergo the political process of choosing a spokesman to deal with the federal agencies and Congress and also to carry on negotiations between the respective groups. It was impossible to simply coalesce around economic deprivation without taking into account cultural differences.

Today the arena of intergroup relations is littered with victims. A tremendous backlash has been built into the white community which need not have existed. Tensions between the different racial and ethnic groups have become unbearable. Communities polarize at the least sign of disorder. All this need not have been.

In particular, the pitfalls of the last two years should have been avoided by the Mexican and Indian communities. The change urged by the Black Power philosophy is not new to Chicanos and Indians. The concept of the groups (be it Black Power, Red Power, or Chicano Power) is a mere duplication of what Indians and Mexicans already had in "The Tribe" and "La Raza."

Many of us fell into the trap of thinking that power movements in the Indian and Mexican communities were new attempts to revitalize the communities. We shortly realized our error. "Power" became synonymous with demagoguery, and it became more important to scare people than to communicate with them. Power, we came to realize, was creating and educating the local community so that it can move forward as a people fully cognizant of themselves. Moreover the reaction of people within the Indian and Mexican communities was sophisticated compared with the reception which *Black Power* received in the white community. Conservatives scaled every wall in the land. For them it became a naked endorsement of violence. "Law and order" became code words for the suppression of the aspirations of the minority groups. Few conservatives recognized that Black Power was the basic philosophy of states' rights which they had worshipped for years. Power spoke against the concentration of policy-making and initiative in one superstructure. Set in the context of a local minority community, conservatives could not understand power and so they feared it.

Perversion of the philosophy of power may have damaged society beyond recall in our generation. While the primary emphasis of the originators of the theory was to build viable communities with political and economic power, the spectacular nature of threats and violence grabbed the imagination and fears of the diverse elements of society and turned the movement into a contest between demagogues. People wishing to support genuine local movements often desired that the local movements be confrontation-oriented so that maximum fund-raising and publicity could be used. The result was that minority groups were handed over to unresponsible prestige-seeking individuals who had personal interests at stake.

We need an immediate reassessment of our contemporary situation in terms of a philosophy of self-determination as expressed in *Black Power*. Perhaps it will have to be called something different. The symbolism of "power" has been worn thin and serves only to block communication at the present time. What are some of the immediate changes we can make by understanding the philosophy of *Black Power*? Can self-determination have a validity as a principle of intergroup relations that will help us meet various crises that may lie ahead? Will the racial problems be solved by the integration of individual members of the respective minority groups into the mainstream of American society? Most people in minority groups are not really convinced that such a mainstream really exists. Can we continue to struggle for justice on an atomistic premise that society is merely a conglomerate of individuals who fall under the same set of laws?

American society has never recognized that groups exist. Yet they have always existed. For centuries the great melting-pot theory was used to explain the apparent creation of a homogeneous society. This theory was accepted because, as Michael Harrington pointed out in *The Other America*, the poor were invisible. Because there was no visible poverty problem, no one challenged the assumption that all whites had been melted. The racial minorities were just as invisible. So people assumed that eventually they would melt also. America was going to be one big happy family. But it never happened. Instead, the gap between white America and the minority groups became greater and greater.

Once we have rejected this melting pot, we can arrive at new definitions of social problems. In recognizing the integrity of the group we can understand the necessity for negotiations between groups. Thus, the self-interest which each group has, and which the respective groups present in their own terms, can be correctly communicated to society as a whole. Perhaps on this basis we can finally arrive at a society of laws and justice. The primary obstacle at present is the unwillingness or inability of the peoples of Western European descent to give up the idea that we are all the same—in every respect. They must learn to understand life in a number of ways from many points of view. And they must understand that each point of view is ultimately related to each other point of view in a number of important ways.

Every fall we see competition between the Scandinavians and

the Italians as to who discovered America. The Scandinavians want Leif Ericson acknowledged as the discoverer of America, while the Italians maintain that Christopher Columbus accomplished the feat. Some Indians want October 11th celebrated as "Indians Discovered Leif Ericson and Christopher Columbus Day." Each group is correct—from their point of view—since their experiences actually began with these men. The fundamental problem raised by this dilemma concerns the history of America. When does it start, from whose point of view is it to be seen, and what does it really mean?

If we are to ease the tensions between groups, then we must be prepared to make radical changes in our bureaucratic and political structures. First and foremost is the replacement of the structure itself with organizations and programs devised by the particular minority group. One aspect of change in this area would be the replacement of nongroup members by group members in those programs which minister most intimately to specific groups. This would mean that decisions affecting certain groups would be made by the people of those groups.

The civil rights components of the Justice Department should be staffed primarily with minority-group people. Policemen in the ghettos, barrios, and reservations should be residents of those areas. Teachers and administrators serving the people in those areas should also be members of the group. In that way ultimate responsibility would be placed on the group to respond to their own needs. People occupying leadership positions in the group would have to be chosen by the group and would not be regarded as outsiders imposing a strange system on the community.

At this point the traditional co-optation process is very dangerous. It can destroy the progress of the group because it seeks to think and act for the group through individuals who are pulled to the edge of the community.

The War on Poverty as it affected Indian reservations is a good example of co-optation and more particularly preemption of leadership. In 1965 there was a massive national funding of certain universities to provide technical assistance for reservation people. A great many staff and policy-making positions were created. Indian college graduates came into these positions when they became aware of the opportunity to work with their own people. At first they were given responsible positions, but when their ideas failed to coincide with those of the universities, they were quickly silenced or released.

Since 1965 Indians have been largely replaced with non-Indians. Programs have become more efficient because they no longer relate to the needs of the reservation people. The War on Poverty has become another bureaucracy because it has been understood by non-Indians as a structure to be administered rather than an opportunity to try innovative ideas for solving poverty problems.

The War on Poverty was not, to my way of thinking, supposed to be an efficient machine that would devour the poor. Rather, it was to be the first effort to work on the problems of economically depressed communities as those communities defined their problems. The Office of Economic Opportunity was supposed to be a frontier-breaking thrust into unexplored fields. It became a funding agency for Head Start, an "experience" for VISTAS with an insatiable longing to help someone, and a chance for bureaucrats to travel the nation crying over the plight of the poor.

The War on Poverty could have been the experimental field for the creation of parallel institutions of which *Black Power* speaks. But when any project appeared to have the potential to fulfill this function, it was quickly squelched. One of the great early ventures was the Child Development Group of Mississippi. CDGM was widely regarded as a significant breakthrough in education by the blacks of that state. But it proved too controversial for the Office of Economic Opportunity and became involved in the political battles between liberals and conservatives in the Senate and funding was cut off.

Indian tribes already had parallel institutions in most cases. Thus they were ready to fund programs as soon as the War on Poverty was announced. Tribes had been self-governing entities fully capable of waging war, entering into treaties, conducting commerce with other nations, and policing themselves for centuries before the white men came. This basic sovereignty lasted into the closing years of the last century.

From the late 1880s until 1934, self-government of Indian tribes was held in limbo as the federal government exercised complete control over the lives and property of Indian people. Such activity was thought to be justified by the outbreaks inspired by Indian religious prophets in the 1890s, which resulted in the Ghost Dance and the Wounded Knee Massacre. Thus every effort was made to destroy Indian culture in order to break the hold of the tribe over individual Indians. It was thought that in this manner peace and quiet would be brought to the frontier.

Indian children were kidnapped and taken thousands of miles away to government boarding schools. Once there, they were whipped if they used their native languages or made any references to their former mode of life. All religious ceremonies were banned on Indian reservations. Priceless objects of art were destroyed on the advice of missionaries and bureaucrats because these were thought to be manifestations of the old pagan way of life. It was a time of forced obliteration of native culture and belief. People thought that by banning everything Indian they could bring the individual Indians from Stone Age to Electric Age in one generation.

Missionaries came to the native village of Kake, Alaska, in 1926. For years they harassed the natives to make them burn all of their totem poles. The totem pole fulfills many functions in native life in Alaska. The figures illustrate historic events and legends that have a real relevancy in the ongoing life of the people. Sometimes they are erected as a memorial to the honored dead of the village. Other times they explain events of the distant past. They are comparable, perhaps, to the coat of arms which is held in high esteem by Europeans. The Christians had mistaken the poles for pagan idols which, of course, was not true. So after the village elders had been pressured for years, the village finally decided to burn its wooden monuments.

In 1969, after a period of forty years during which white society had achieved a certain sense of maturity, the missionaries decided that they had been wrong in having the poles burned, so they encouraged the people to build new ones.

The tragedy of Kake has been reflected many times in the histories of the minority groups. Always, it seems, ignorant and immature whites who happen to be in positions of power make decisions that vitally affect the lives of people in minority groups. They always appear to be acting in goodwill, but there is always a tendency for them to make decisions on the basis of their beliefs and information rather than to allow the local people to solve their own problems in their own way.

In 1934 the Indian tribes received the benefits of the Indian Reorganization Act. This law gave them the basic rights of self-government on the reservations. Under IRA, the reservations were organized as federal corporations. Tribes were subject only to the approval of the Secretary of the Interior on certain major decisions affecting tribal and individual property. In almost every other area tribes were allowed to begin building parallel institutions.

Tribes have done extremely well under the Indian Reorganization Act. With their own law-and-order programs they have greatly eased the friction between themselves and the neighboring white communities off reservation. In spite of some shortcomings in administration, there has been more justice for Indian people in tribal courts than there would have been had everyone been under the control of non-Indians residing off the reservations.

In 1954 there was a massive effort to place Indian communities under the civil and criminal jurisdiction of the states. Congress unilaterally placed certain tribes under state jurisdiction and gave broad approval to states to amend their constitutions to enable them to provide police services to reservations. Most of the western states were admitted to the union under restrictive clauses which forbade them to exercise any jurisdiction over the lives and property of Indian people residing on the respective reservations.

The net result of the attempt by the states to assume civil and criminal jurisdiction was the creation of "no man's lands" on the reservations. States were ceded jurisdiction by the federal government but they simply refused to provide any law for Indian people. And the federal government disclaimed any further responsibility for Indian reservations.

Parallel institutions for other minority groups should be created with a definite legal status as quickly as possible if we are to avoid total collapse of the political system. William Strickland, Vice-Chairman of the Columbia Broadcasting Company, told a seminar on "Black Politics and Ghetto Economics" at the University of Colorado last year that revolution was inevitable and that it would come as a result of the clash of antagonistic interests. He insisted that black people must develop their own political system rather than try to work through the existing political system, which he labeled "totally irrelevant."

If groups work out their own mode of political expression *internal to their group*, then as a group they can relate to the Constitutional framework and the national political scheme will not be irrelevant to each group. So long as groups are visible and vocal but have no status in and of themselves within the political system, there is no conceivable way that the present system can be relevant to them. The present system is built upon individual expression and has no place for group expression—with the exception again of Indian tribes.

There are a substantial number of people within minority groups who desire peaceful change. At the same time that the Kerner Report was concluding that America was still splitting into two separate and unequal societies, Flora Lewis of *Newsday* was reporting a new militancy among blacks for peace and integration. She quoted Mrs. Myrtle Whitmore, manager of a low-cost housing project in East Harlem, to the effect that the excesses of the militants have created a desire by local blacks to speak for themselves. Some are beginning to refuse to have militants speak for them. This "implosion," as Joseph Kraft called it, has hit all minority groups in the last year. National leaders have been wiped out by developments on the local scene and now local militants are being replaced by community reactions to their tactics.

Already the emphasis is beginning to shift to economic development, but here again thinking has been sparse and old fashioned. People supporting black capitalism have been accused of wanting to create local barons, thereby letting the mass of people continue to starve. Little thought has been given to the creation of new forms of holding and developing capital. I believe that "power" goals will continue to remain with us for some time. They will be expressed in a variety of goals and programs. Until a center around which expressions of power can be integrated is found, minority groups will continue to flounder. White America will continue to get upset at every development within the different minority groups, for it will consider them threats to traditional ways of doing business.

With the continual threat of co-optation facing minority groups as they are presently constituted, it is imperative that the basic sovereignty of the minority group be recognized. This would have the immediate effect of placing racial minorities in a negotiating position as a group and would nullify co-optation. While there would be the constant desire to co-opt, the chances of such behavior would be lessened and a balance of power could be achieved through political alliances. Recognition of new interpretations of the Constitution based on the concept of the group would be the vital step in this process.

7 * POWER, SOVEREIGNTY, AND FREEDOM

MUCH of the emphasis of recent years has been toward the realization of power by segments of the minority communities. Power has been defined in a number of ways, and where it has not been defined, activism has been substituted for power itself. Thus decibel level has often passed for elucidation and voluminous sloganizing has replaced articulation of ideas.

In 1966, a number of us in the Indian field advanced "Red Power" as a means of putting the establishment on. We were greatly surprised when newspapermen began to take us seriously and even more so when liberals who had previously been cool and unreceptive began to smile at us in conferences. But the militant medium was quick to overtake us. Consequently I was approached one day in a Midwestern city by a group of young Indians who asked for my permission to break windows. Red Power had arrived!

The very concept of power has been so debilitated in recent

years that it now seems incongruous to speak of mere power when the younger and more aggressive people are threatening to burn everything down. Yet power cannot be understood outside of its social-political context. When merged together, the social and political aspects ultimately become historical-religious concepts describing movement by a particular group of people toward a particular destiny. Few members of racial minority groups have realized that inherent in their peculiar experience on this continent is hidden the basic recognition of their power and sovereignty.

The white man has systematically excluded and deprived the racial minorities, so that to speak of a minority group immediately calls to mind a certain profile of the oppressed. Behind this profile stands both the victim and the oppressor and their motivations which have created the oppression and the reaction to it. If we are to understand power in its creative modern sense, we must probe the characters and their attitudes to find the principle of exclusion which has barred the groups from participation in the economic life of the nation.

Discrimination in the case of blacks and deprivation of culture in the case of the American Indian and Mexican American has been built upon a tacit recognition of the "groupness" of these communities. That is to say, discrimination and deprivation were not founded on the dislikes of the white community for any particular individual in the minority groups. Rather these attitudes were based upon the fear of and dislike of the groups because they were groups. Insofar as they had identity, that peculiar identity was the red flag waved before the white bull.

Indian tribes face tremendous Congresssional pressure to sell their land, divide the assets, and disperse. Blacks were systematically excluded from educational opportunities, from white restaurants, from motels and hotels, specifically because they were black. Where members of minority groups have "crossed over," they have been able to go from identification with one group to another, at least symbolically and secretly.

Because discrimination has been based upon group identity, it has been through group action that progress has been made toward making the political structure more flexible. Or, in the case of Indian tribes, group action by coalitions of tribes have enabled the Indian community to withstand the incredible pressures brought to bear on them. When one reverses the powerlessness of the minority groups and begins to affirm the handicaps suffered by minority groups as positive aspects of their place in American society, the emergence of certain concepts becomes quite clear.

Powerlessness becomes potential for power within certain limits using certain techniques. Scapegoat identity becomes sovereignty of the group and freedom from oppression because of race, color, or culture becomes a positive identity which can be fulfilled rather than a hurdle to be overcome. This is the threat over and above the burning and looting which frightens all white Americans. When the position of the minority groups is viewed in its philosophical and conceptual positive sense, then it is clear that ONLY minority groups can have an identity which will withstand the pressures and the tidal waves of the electric world. ONLY minority groups have within themselves the potential for exercise of power. And ONLY minority groups have the vision of freedom before them. For this reason, at Woodstock in 1969, the disenchanted white youth proclaimed themselves a new minority group.

While merely announcing the formation of a new minority group does not make it so, yet the willingness to identify as a separate and distinct group in the face of four centuries of Western European tradition on this continent and two centuries of persecution of minority groups by the United States government indicates that something lasting may be afoot. The next few years may well tell whether white society itself will break apart into irreconcilable groups, or whether the present movement by youth is another fad to fill the leisure of affluence.

Much of the significance of group movement today is that leadership within the respective groups is taking the reverse side of the coin of discrimination and emphasizing the positive side of discriminatory concepts. But far too few leaders are willing to realize the philosophical implications of the reversal. In many cases they are using derogatory terms tagged on their group years ago by an uneducated white majority as proofs of racism inherent in the white man, rather than using the stone rejected by the builders to form a new edifice.

Persecution of a group because it is a group is the negative side of that group's existence. And such values have validity only when the persecuting majority has a united front. In today's white world no such front exists. It therefore seems unfair and a method of copping out to continually call on minority groups to fight white racism. Such efforts merely polarize whites against minority groups without taking into account the need of minority groups to solidify themselves for positive and aggressive action.

In order to validate the persecution of a group, the persecutors must in effect recognize the right of that group to be different. And if the group is different in a lasting sense, then it can be kept as a scapegoat for the majority. It also suffers with respect to its deviations—blacks as to color, Indians and Mexicans as to culture. The question is then posed as to how far the deviations fall short of the white norm and how far they indicate the basic solidity and validity of the group.

Implicit in the sufferings of each group is the acknowledgment of the sovereignty of the group. It is this aspect—sovereignty—which has never been adequately used by minority groups to their own advantage. Perhaps many cannot conceive of sovereignty outside of a territory within which they can exercise their own will. But with the present scene strewn with victims of violence, many of the victims intruders on the turf of the local communities, this cannot be the case.

More to the point, perhaps, is the fact that legal issues have always been presented in the singular—is such and such a violation of the basic rights of the individual? Thus the attention of the minority groups has been drawn away from their rights and power as a group to a quicksand of assimilationist theories which destroy the power of the group to influence its own future, when that future is dominated by continued persecution of individuals because of their group membership.

Tactical efforts of minority groups should be based upon the concept of sovereignty. Only in this manner can they hope to affect policies which now block them from full realization of the nature and extent of their problems. And the history of intergroup relations is littered with examples of the recognition, no matter how implicit, of the sovereignty of minority groups.

Any leader in a minority-group community will inevitably have it thrown at him that he "doesn't represent all the (blacks, Indians, Mexicans, etc.)." Why should he? What is it in the mind of whites, sympathetic and hostile, that demands that the leadership in a minority community represent ALL the people in that community when the questioner represents NONE of his community? Even under the most rudimentary reading of the Constitution, only a majority is required for whites to represent themselves. Yet an absolute majority is always required of minority groups in order for them to have a valid opinion.

This demand is a recognition of the fundamental sovereignty of the group. It basically states that the group is foreign and autonomous, whether it actually is or not, and that whites can have no dealing with a segment of that community on the chance that they will take the wrong group and find themselves in trouble. This recognition of the basic integrity of the minority-group community has been used in a negative sense to play politics within the group and neutralize them. It should now be seen in a positive sense as an affirmation, in spite of the flowery phrases of equality and unity, of the basic position of the group as a sovereign, autonomous nation which must be treated as an equal entity to the federal and state governments.

When sovereignty is combined with power on behalf of the community, then it becomes apparent that power is manifested in a major way by the willingness to enter into agreements between communities. Without formalized agreements or treaties, there is no way that two communities can work together if one community insists on recognizing the sovereignty of the other, even though it denies the abstract validity of the other as a sovereign community.

In the field of job placement and employment this dilemma is most clearly evident. Individuals are turned down because of racial reasons. Yet the white community continues to act as if the black community were sovereign and should be able to demand a certain percentage of available jobs as its "quota." Externally the rhetoric is equality for individuals. In practice, the tendency is discrimination of alarming proportions against individual members of the group.

One of the major areas of concern between whites and minority groups has always been the field of education. Countless millions have been invested in minority-group programs to develop "leaders" for the respective communities. If there was not a tacit recognition of the basic sovereignty of the group, would it be necessary to develop leaders for the group? Abstract individualism of Western European man needs no leadership for divergent groups.

History has shown that such leadership is generally assassinated, lest it prove destructive of the governmental structure.

Some of the most famous and many of the infamous programs foisted upon minority groups in recent years, however, have been "leadership-training" programs in which the cream of the crop is siphoned off to become a colonial elite which will do the bidding of the white majority and somehow lead the community into the fold of the white man. Yet when the leadership tries to do precisely that, the community itself is rejected. Black leaders of recent years are classic examples of this inconsistency. Most were well educated. Martin Luther King, Jr., had a doctorate in religion and could have been considered the finest product of Western cultural and educational processes as they affect leadership potential in the minority groups. Yet when King attempted to put into practice the very lessons, theological and religious, which he had studied at the feet of the wisest of the white Western world, he was immediately classified as an "outside agitator" with suspected Communist leanings.

Blacks have recently come to the fore with attacks on the white desire to create a black Moses. They have rightly pointed out that such programs and goals neglect the mass of the community in favor of creating one or two favored and powerful individuals. Bur can anyone seriously think that minority groups are so dumb as not to recognize the place of Moses in the life of the Hebrew people? Can the Moses archetype, therefore, be anything but a call to the minority groups to create their own religions, political systems, economic concerns, and culture?

Moses took a loose confederation of tribal people, stuck in industrialized urban Egypt, and brought them out of Egypt after totally destroying the country. He then formed a much broader conception of religion based upon their experiences in that urban society, and reconstituted the tribal structure with religion as the basis. So strong was the tribal-religious interpretation of identity, that the people of Israel have lasted nearly four thousand years and show no signs of weakening.

Leadership training is thus the implicit recognition of the fundamental sovereignty of a group. But it is more than simply sovereignty. It posits the struggle with oppressive forces and victory over them. It also outlines certain modes of action by which the group can make itself invulnerable while it waits the final victory. In this context, leadership training for minority groups indicates the presence of a suicide complex within the white community—or at the very least, an incredible cultural naïveté that assumes that its values are so overwhelming that they cannot be resisted, much less questioned.

Another indication of the recognition of the sovereignty of minority groups is the perennial question raised in sociological journals by sociological high priests of the urban culture—"WHO SPEAKS FOR THE (blacks, Indians, Mexicans)?" On the practical level this question becomes "Who are your leaders?"

An analysis of the motivation behind this question is revealing. Whites desire to find out who REALLY REPRESENTS the minority communities, feeling that if they can once negotiate their problems with that leader, the problem can be solved. Strangely enough, they also use this question as a gag line expounded by invading Martians, indicating that perhaps they feel that the minority groups are as far removed from humanity as the Martians.

If the white community is willing to deal only with the leaders of minority groups, is not this the best indication that they somehow understand the natural sovereignty of the group? That they are willing and find a need to negotiate with the rightful government of the group? Again, practical behavior betrays all protestations of belief in the validity of individualism as a way of life.

Moynihan and Glazer, in *Beyond the Melting Pot*, point out that the urban concentrations of Western European immigrants suggest an adherence to social forms of the old countries. Vestiges of sovereignty and tribalism still exist, and city life must adapt itself to each group. Rarely does the group conform to the established patterns it finds. More often, it bends existing conditions to fit its particular cultural needs. But that sovereignty is not recognized, since no one takes the time or trouble to inquire who the leaders of the Polish, Swedish, or Irish communities are.

The demonic desire to identify leaders by the power-brokers of white America is a positive indication of their unarticulated feeling that minority groups are inevitably different in a peculiar way. When this desire to locate leaders manifests itself in witch hunts against the dissident white youth, then the status of white youth as a new minority group is assured. They are treated as if they had a government-in-exile, which could become extremely dangerous to the established way of doing business if given half the chance.

Most of the trials being conducted against rioters, demonstrators, and students are posited upon the assumption that a few leaders were able to influence the masses to do what they wanted. Thus articulate spokesmen who could give voice and meaning to the movement experienced by the dissidents are tagged "conspirators," and charges are made against them. In the Chicago trials which came as a result of the disturbances during the Democratic Convention, the farce is apparent.

A national report characterized the Chicago disturbances as a "police riot." Trying Jerry Rubin and others for inciting a police riot may be politically pleasing, but it is no less ludicrous. It basically affirms that all who follow certain preordained patterns of behavior belong to and have rights under the federal Constitution. All others are deviant minority groups with a basic right to sovereignty and independence.

If force and repression are the only responses to divergent viewpoints, it appears inevitable that traditional conceptions of society will break down completely and society itself will be reduced to a cultural and political truce between groups characterized as minority and dissident. Hence, the more intense the oppression and the more numerous the witchhunts after "leaders" of the various conspiracies, the faster society alienates its creative thinkers and concerned people. Law and order is the way to destruction.

A good example of this tendency is the persecution of Ken Kesey and Timothy Leary during the early days of acid. Feeling that the two constituted the "leadership" of the acid generation, the power structure undertook to destroy them in the hopes that it could avert the spread of drugs among the youth. All that was accomplished was the rapid development of a separate and distinct drug culture with acid-rock music and a determination to survive.

Sovereignty and power go hand in hand in group action. One cannot exist without the other, although either can be misused to the detriment of the other. Thus power without a concept of responsibility to a sovereign group is often ruthlessness in disguise. Thus the attempt by foundations and churches to "give" power to the powerless has resulted in the creation and support of demagogues and not the transfer of power, since power cannot be given and accepted.

The responsibility which sovereignty creates is oriented primarily toward the existence and continuance of the group. As such, it naturally creates a sense of freedom not possible in any other context. Freedom has traditionally meant an absence of restrictions. The fact that passports are not needed to go from state to state is often cited as an example of the freedoms which we have in this country that are not present in other nations.

This is too naïve to hold much water, however. If freedom is to be defined in counterdistinction to oppression, then people are free to the extent that they do not feel immediate oppression or they do not recognize alternatives to oppression. In this sense a failure to enforce laws would be as valid as an absence of laws itself. This is the sense of individual and group freedom shared by the early hippies. The refusal to follow traditional norms was considered a breakthrough for freedom of the group.

In the years since the massive hippie migrations to the Haight and other centers of the acid culture, the power structure has become aware of the irresponsibility toward laws and has cracked down on the youth. Thus the initial freedom of the hippie was due more toward a lack of energy on the part of the Establishment than to the discovery of a new way of life by the hippies.

With the emergence of the Woodstock Nation and the absolute failure of the police to enforce laws against them during the festival, people are becoming optimistic about the creation of a lasting culture of the new minority group. This cannot be unless the individuals articulating the sovereignty of the new group find within their own understanding the necessity to be responsible to the group itself. If this is developed, then the freedom which sovereignty can give will emerge within the group.

The freedom of sovereignty is based upon the passage beyond traditional stumbling blocks of Western man. It is existence beyond the problem of identity and power conflicts. Buffy Sainte-Marie has a classic phrase to characterize this freedom. She says that an Indian doesn't have to dress or act like an Indian because he already is one. This is the freedom of sovereignty without which sovereignty itself cannot exist.

In certain areas of action in the minority groups and post-hippie movement such freedom currently exists. Many people are fellow-sympathizers without putting on the costume of the hippie of yesterday or the nationalist of today. They fully share the mores and ideas of the group without finding it necessary to conform to the outward aspects of dress and action in order to claim identity.

For a long time liberals held this pattern of freedom within their community. A man might not necessarily have to participate in activities of the liberal community so long as he raised his voice and exerted his individual strength on behalf of his beliefs when the crisis came. It was during the later days of the civil rights movement that this aspect of liberalism was destroyed. People demanded that everyone go all the way in everything or be tagged racists. Thus the sovereignty of the liberal community was destroyed because the freedom beyond the identity crisis was denied to people.

One of the chief weaknesses of the Indian community has been its absolute freedom. Like the liberal freedom described above, Indian people were free to participate according to their own sense of responsibility. In massing to prevent an invasion of rights, Indians were often able to come up with a very meager fighting force because the cause was not attractive enough. No individual was forced to participate in any course of action since he was freed from allegiance to abstractions.

Freedom in this context begins with certain tribal assumptions which are not questioned, since they would not provide answers capable of articulation. An Indian never questions whether or not he is an Indian. The query he faces is *what kind* of Indian. And this is the same question now facing individuals of other groups which affirmed the sovereignty of their group.

Living beyond the identity question channels behavior patterns into a tacit acknowledgment of the customs of the group. Thus the problem of law and order which plagues urbanized Western society does not have the fear potential and impact in sovereign groups. Competition is limited to group values and has the welfare of the people as a group as its reference point. To impose restrictions from outside and define freedom in that manner would undercut the values of the group.

The contemporary struggle between the younger and older generations may be a manifestation of the clash between two understandings of freedom. While the older generation still suffers from nightmares of its European past where arbitrary exercise of police powers created a rigid society and persecutions, it can only conceive of freedom as a lack of restrictions imposed from outside the group. Its only choice to maintain a relatively safe existence is to grasp power and manipulate it for the benefit of those who are acceptable in that particular generation.

Youth and minority groups conceive of freedom as an unfilled potential of being. They despise rules and regulations which compress the individual into a state of fear and conformity. The difference is easy to see. The older generation tries to be "good," that is, it wants to live without a police record and with plenty of recommendations. Youth tries to "be," that is, to express what it feels as a result of being a person. Therefore police records and acceptance by society are nice but not really relevant to the question of freedom.

The way of youth and minority groups is the more difficult path of the two. It is ultimately dependent upon the existence of the group and its ability to use its power constructively. There is thus great danger that immoral use of group power or unwitting compromise will destroy the sovereignty of the group and dissipate the power, thus turning fundamental freedoms into licentiousness.

At this stage in history it is vitally important that power movements, insofar as they do represent movements toward sovereignty, are viewed in that light. The unreasonable fear which affirmation of sovereignty creates when it is not understood is not worth the effort. Globally, efforts to assert sovereignty have been universally interpreted as a gigantic plot against Western man. Thus the Vietnam civil war has become an insidious Communist movement of global import. People feel that unless the Vietcong are stopped in the Mekong Delta, they will soon invade Westchester County. Patriots of the old order volunteer for Vietnam stating that they would much rather stop the Communists over there than in Disneyland.

From the lack of understanding of the movement toward sovereignty of numerous nation groups comes the understanding of the world which again recognizes the enemy as a sovereign group. Thus Communism is viewed as a massive and monolithic threat against all that is decent. From this premise, every disturbance regardless of its original motivation, is lumped into the the universal conspiracy.

This viewpoint is destructive in every aspect. It allows a "cowboy-and-Indian" interpretation, the good guys of peaceful settlement against the bad guys of the uprising, of every major event. With data transmission being instantaneous, there is no possibility of transcending the specific events to find a more realistic understanding of the nature of the world. Fear created by lack of understanding thus increases geometrically, and force is brought to bear in an effort to combat the imagined threat.

The natural result of this type of conflict is the opposition of abstract mythology against events of the real world. Events are not understood in their own context, but they are categorized according to preconceived interpretations of the world. When this situation is combined with the optimistic conception of history as "progress" which has been the standard of distinction used by Western man, the result is truly demonic and frightening. Western man thus is creating his own barbaric tribes which, when faced with continual alienation and misunderstanding, desire nothing more than the total destruction of Western society.

An examination of some of the conflicts on the global level will indicate the variety of movements of people toward a basic sovereignty of their group. If most of the conflicts are viewed in a sovereign context, policies can be reordered to fit local needs and a certain flexibility can be achieved. There is no reason why groups cannot declare their social, cultural, and religious independence if it will support the aspirations of their group. In doing so they would strengthen their primary political and economic allegiance and useless conflict could be avoided.

One of the major problems of Canada has been the continual conflict between French-speaking and English-speaking peoples. When the Canadian government was trying to put through constitutional reforms in late 1968, there was a tremendous flap over the use of certain words. Prime Minister Jean-Jacques Beartand of Quebec wanted to change the name of the province's main lawmaking body from "Legislative Assembly" to "National Assembly of the Province of Quebec."

Mere use of the word "nation" created a situation of serious concern. The English took the word to refer only to Canada as a sovereign nation. The French took it as an acknowledgment of the French-speaking Canadian community. Thus while the word satisfied the French nationalists of Quebec, explicit recognition of the sovereignty of the French of Quebec province sent the English peoples into a panic at the thought of a divided Canada.

No recognition was made by the English citizens that Quebec was separate in every sense but formal political ties. While Pierre Trudeau was able to postpone any split, the election highlighted the issues between French and English which go back to the days when the two European nations were busy fighting each other for the right to rape North America.

Robert Stanfield, Trudeau's opponent, tried to win French Quebec's support by affirming the principle that Canada was the result of two founding peoples. Stanfield's followers argued that the word "nation" meant in reality "people" and not "state." Thus the issues were never joined. Trudeau spoke of political structure, while his opponents spoke of cultural sovereignty—Quebec as the homeland of a distinctive people—the French-Canadians.

If Canada can resolve this dispute by acknowledging the right of the French people to maintain a cultural and social sovereignty with its corresponding sense of freedom and power, it will be able to lay this dispute to rest. By doing so it will solve the political turmoil in which it seems destined to become enmeshed.

As if the Canadian problem was not enough, similar troubles exist in Louisiana with the Acadians. Two hundred years ago, during the wars between France and England, the English forced the Acadians out of Nova Scotia and drove them southward into exile in Louisiana. Longfellow was not able to provide them with as good an image as he did Hiawatha, and so many people have forgotten they they continue to exist.

For centuries a cultural battle was waged against the Acadians by the state of Louisiana to make them give up the French language and learn English. Here again was a clash of cultures which was supposed to be solved by forceful oppression of the minority culture. In 1968 legislation a council was created to develop French in Louisiana. A law was passed making French mandatory in elementary and secondary schools. The University of Southwestern Louisiana held a six-week course in teaching local French.

This is another case where the basic sovereignty of an ethnic group was maintained by the people for three centuries of separation from the mother country, with the group continuing to assert itself. The very existence of the Acadians of Louisiana should be eloquent testimony to the persistence of communal-tribal groups and their intent to remain as an identifiable community with a will of their own. Whither goest the melting pot?

Three centuries is not a long time, however, for a tribalistic group to maintain itself. The Basques of Spain have maintained themselves as a distinct group ever since anyone can remember. Their origin is lost in the mists of time. They have simply always been around. And they have always been political activists. It is said that although they represent only 5 percent of the population of Spain, they account for 95 percent of the political terrorism against Franco.

If the white middle class is upset about the black desire to form a separate state or the Indian desire to maintain reservations, they would be driven crazy by the Basques. Basques of separatist persuasion want to make a separate nation of three northern provinces of Spain. Behind this drive is the same basic question which sets many Indian tribes on edge.

For some years beginning in 1925 Basques were permitted to collect taxes in their provinces and pay a fixed fee to the Spanish government each year. They then used the remainder of the money to do what they wished. They thus had created a fundamental autonomy over their provinces and exercised self-government. Franco is stuck right in the middle of this problem and has no viable alternatives so long as the use of force to suppress the Basques is advocated.

If Franco restores the tax privilege, he can be accused of failing to keep the Basques under control. If he continues to oppress the Basques, he merely spreads the sense of alienation and dissatisfaction further throughout Spain. Again, a political solution is presented as the answer to a cultural problem. The basic sovereignty of the Basque provinces is their fighting point, and short of a change of understanding of the nature of groups there can be no answer for Spain.

Economic and political problems affecting the sovereignty of groups are minor compared to the problems between the Catholics and Protestants in Northern Ireland. After centuries of discrimination because of religious differences, fighting finally broke out in 1969. Some places in northern Ireland have fences separating the two groups. The tension is incredible. People are identified by their religious orientation and discrimination is on a religious basis. But it is nonetheless discrimination. And the Catholics are none the less making their religious independence a cause which affects all areas of life in Ireland.

With tempers rising to a high pitch, it may be that a religious compromise with equal status for both groups can be the only solution. Certainly in this situation overlooking the basic integrity of the two communities and pretending that group differences do not exist will be fatal to any chance of decreasing tensions and solving the problem. When American minority groups achieve their own post-Christian religions, the same type of conflict will break out between mainstream white America which never did pay any attention to Christianity and the minority communities which have developed a religious life.

As the conflict develops in Ireland, we must pay attention to the events and issues brought forth. Theocratic sovereignty is no less sovereignty. It is an attempt to carry forward into modern times the mythology of Western man. While it may be possible to do so in Ireland, it is no longer possible to do so in America. The struggle in Ireland thus previews for us what we will face unless concepts are radically changed to provide a status for all deviant groups within our nation.

Foremost in the examples of religious sovereignty is, of course, Israel. The development of modern Israel is prefigured in the history of the Jewish people. While many people of Jewish descent do not accept the establishment of Israel as a valid event in the history of their community, because it is political and not religious, other groups look to the Jews as an example of religious validity. No other religion has had the ability to maintain itself and its community for so long and under such conditions.

One indication of fundamental sovereignty over and above political existence is the renewal of Hebrew as a living language. Kibbutz settlements and urban concentrations (over seventy schools) are concentrating on the teaching of Hebrew as the language of the nation despite the fact that Hebrew has not been used for some two thousand years. Since the Jews are far ahead of other groups, it may be that the desire for an independent language will be one of the next issues faced by minority groups in this country and other nations having existing minority groups.

Certain black groups have tried Swahili and other African languages as a means of increasing their drive for separate status. On some reservations Indian languages are now taught and the end of this movement is not in sight. And certainly the drive of French groups, as already discussed, toward revitalization of the French language, indicates that the move toward ethnic and racial separatism has just begun.

As linguistic, economic, religious, social, and cultural drives are integrated into philosophies of action by groups, it will become apparent that the Western world is being submerged in tribalism and ethnic communities. And the sovereignty of each group which is now being maintained and advocated by leaders of the respective groups will have to be acknowledged if the nations of the world are to achieve orderly societies.

Such recognition has previously been denied by the ruling classes because they have refused to consider the implications of group sovereignty on a global basis. Too often they have cast aside movements they did not understand and implied that these were Communist or demonic. Taken in a world context, a great many groups are fighting independently for a distinct legal status, recognition of their community, and the right to conduct all of their local affairs without interference from the centralized and paranoid federal government.

One of the arguments advanced to suppress local autonomy of

separatist tribal groups is that the individuals of the respective groups would suffer brutality and discrimination by their leaders if the groups were given full independence. Such a charge is not only poppycock, but reveals a lack of understanding of the nature of tribal-communal societies. It also assumes that the people within minority groups are presently receiving preferred treatment by law-enforcement officers, which would be taken away if they were given power over their own lives.

The Black Muslims have suffered this accusation many times. Yet few people take the time to realize that the Muslims have created a society that is much better than the assimilated groups around them and that certainly has a more humane social system than America itself. Respect for individuals within the group is a noted trait of the Black Muslims. Their desire for a separate state is predicated upon their drive for economic independence within twenty or twenty-five years. In every respect except official legal status, the Black Muslims have succeeded in creating their own nation within a nation.

Another group which has maintained itself in spite of intense pressures to disband, and which can be said to have created its own nation, are the Amish of the Midwest. Devoutly religious, they have banded together in a theocracy and then expanded this basic religious belief into a comprehensive way of life. Amish are never on the welfare rolls, they maintain farms and businesses of exemplary stature. The only conflict which they have is in the field of education, and it is a desperate conflict.

One would think that a people who are absolutely no burden on the public, who have better social profiles than the society in which they live, and who contribute a great deal to their immediate locale would be welcomed by society as an example of proper social adjustment. Such is not the case. The newspapers featured pictures several years back of burly Iowa troopers chasing frightened little Amish children through the cornfields trying to force them to go to public schools.

Through education, every effort is being made to break the Amish society and "merge" them with the grand and glorious mainstream of America where the divorce rate is approaching 50 percent, where the crime rate continues to skyrocket, and where education is as relevant as the surface temperature of Jupiter is to the Eskimos of the North.

In the middle of 1969 there was a considerable flap between the Amish of Indiana and the state officials concerning the use of reflectors on vehicles. State law required certain shapes and colors. The Amish refused to use these since they regarded them as a violation of their religious beliefs. While the Amish won the battle on color, the case has not been solved with respect to the shape of the reflectors.

In a fit of flexibility and understanding, Floyd Kline, Director of the State Office of Traffic Safety, was reported to have said, "I'll go along with them on the new colors. That's for religious reasons and Lord knows, there's too little religion in the world as it is. But I'll fight anyone about the identifying shape. I'm going to be quite adamant about that."

Using political power to attempt to make a cultural group conform to some abstract and irrelevant pattern seems about as immature as can be. In this incident one can see that the desire of the power structure is not for order or understanding. It is pure naked and arbitrary exercise of force to make a group surrender its beliefs so as to conform to another cultural interpretation of the world. And the group persecuted, the Amish, have adequately demonstrated, even by the standards of white society, that their way of life is infinitely better than that of their persecutors.

Can people even be serious about justice, equality, and order when this type of behavior goes on? Would it not be better to create a special legal status for groups such as the Amish, one which would recognize their right to live as they please within a larger Constitutional context? If not, American society may well fall over the dispute on the shape of reflectors or some other eternal and ultimate question.

Among the other dissident groups splitting from American society, the most publicized are the hippie alumni. They had, by summer of 1969, become the largest group of new landowners in northern New Mexico. Deserting the urban slums and desiring to create a new type of life in rural areas, hundreds of former flower children came to New Mexico to set up independent communes. The movement has spread and now some communes have been established in the eastern United States in the forested areas of New England. But these are dwarfed by the development of urban communes and pads.

In almost every case the movement is toward withdrawal and establishment of sovereign groups. With corresponding development of internal customs of each group and new religious practices, the establishment of the new minority group will be complete. It will remain only for them to begin to exercise their untouched power as a group on the political processes of the nation, and then they will have achieved almost total independence and the freedom which sovereignty and independence can give.

One indication that this movement may be for real are the continued reports of serious involvement with artistic projects and cultural activities by the alumni of the hippie movement in the North Beach area of San Francisco. North Beach appears to be making a comeback as an area in which cultural pioneers are pulling the present generation away from the despair of the beatniks, the euphoria of the flower children, and the disasters of the politically active for intensive creative examination of the present state of society.

The trend toward independence by minority, ethnic, and youth groups appears to be just starting. The days of power movements and demonstrations may be over. If so, the nature of the problem of dissident groups and cultural rebels is much more serious than middle-class America realizes. The basic message of demonstrations was that the demonstrators "cared" enough to protest. They had not yet reached the necessity to affirm their sovereignty as a group and to use that sovereignty as a means of withdrawal and boycott.

Now, it appears, traditional Western culture has become largely irrelevant to the needs of a substantial number of people. They would rather fight it out on behalf of their own communities than make any further attempts to conform or reach a cultural compromise with the impotent mythologies of Western man. Oppressive measures will undoubtedly increase, since the power structure now sees an opportunity to crush some of the movements following their withdrawal.

It is absolutely vital to the continuance of any semblance of society for the recognition of groups as groups to be acknowledged. In this way, as groups split off from their allegiance to traditional myths, they will still have a status within the Constitutional framework that will not prove abrasive to other groups or to those people who continue to adhere to the traditional myths.

Unless society can find a means of integrating the rights of groups with the broader and more abstract rights of individuals, it will succeed in creating its own barbarians who will eventually destroy it. Oppressive legislation, once written into law, will come back to haunt the very people who wrote the laws. The sovereignty of tribalistic-communal groups is more than the conglomerate of individual desires writ large. It is a whole new way of adjusting to the technology which dominates life in this century.

If society refuses to adjust to what it has created, it cannot gain the upper hand over developments which are not integrated into a consistent understanding of the world and which have, by almost everyone's agreement, turned man into the object of events which take away from him the power over his world. Sovereignty is dangerous only to the extent that it follows traditional modes of social change which are merely adjustments of the basic structure and not changes at all.

This is not to say that no alternatives can be created by society which will neutralize present developments. Society is basically an expression of Western man. As such, it can at any time revert to traditional hidden forms of social organization which are contained in the historical experience of Western European man. Simple reversion to tribal forms by dissidents against Western cultural forms does not guarantee that the movement will not go beyond tribalism, McLuhan not withstanding, to an ancient feudalistic form which would be more comfortable for the descendants of King Arthur and Charlemagne.

The present situation is thus fraught with desperate alternatives. The question is whether or not the current movements can struggle through the problems now facing them to achieve a new type of society, or whether at the last minute they will relapse into traditional European forms and mankind will be doomed to repeat the history of Western man in a new setting.

8 * THE NEW CONSTITUTION

AT A COLLEGE inauguration ceremony in 1969, McGeorge Bundy, head of the Ford Foundation and former advisor to Presidents Kennedy and Johnson, suggested that the United States may need a new Constitution. Bundy said that the struggle of American society leaves a persistent gulf between our ideals of individual dignity and the reality of equal opportunity. Our behavior, which results in the denial of personal worth and the practice of intense discrimination, is, Bundy noted, "sharper, more bitter, more violent and even perhaps more dangerous than anything we have known since the Civil War."

"It is not unthinkable," Bundy remarked, "that this country may need a new Constitution." But he said also that he would probably vote against a new Constitution if given the chance, because he didn't believe that we could do much better than our forefathers. In conclusion, Bundy placed his hopes in the rising generation to create a new political activism that could move an effective majority for a level of social change unprecedented in our history.

The suggestion that the United States may need a new Constitution stuns many people. The American way of government has proved successful for the majority of whites and amendments to the Constitution have proven helpful to the racial minority groups. There is always a tendency to view the Constitution in terms of the modern world instead of the world in which it was written. Thus we have today the benefit of two centuries of experience in government when we interpret the Constitution—a benefit which the founding fathers did not have. We also have the tremendous legacy of cases interpreting certain principles of law which define for us the meaning of government and individual rights.

There is a great deal in what Bundy has advocated. The Constitution was drawn up by property-owners of the respective states to provide protection for the growing nation and the property interests that would make it successful. The basic orientation of the Constitution has not changed since its adoption; it still protects property, whereas the modern world has made protection of individual rights and definition of the interests of society paramount. In order to better comprehend Bundy's suggestion, we should understand the philosophical principles inherent in the Constitution before we decide on changing it.

The Constitution was devised by a group of people in a particular time and place who were highly influenced by the British Empiricists' political philosophy. In seeking to justify their revolution against established authority and to give the new government an ideology that appeared to be sound, the founding fathers fell back upon the writings of John Locke for their ideas.

John Locke's theory of political organization depended upon the creation of a "social compact" between free men. Under this theory, governments were instituted for the ordering of relationships among the citizenry and little else. In the *Second Essay Concerning the True Original Extent and End of Civil Government*, Locke felt that a government can be constituted

> wherever . . . any number of men so unite into one society as to quit every one his executive power of the law of Nature, and to resign it to the public. . . . And this is done wherever any number of men, in the state of Nature enter into society to make one people one body politic under one supreme government: or else when any one joins himself to, and incorporates with any government already made. For hereby he authorizes the society or which is all one, the legislative thereof, to make laws for him as the public good of the society shall require, to the execution whereof his own assistance is due.

Locke had projected backward in time to a theoretical dawn of history to find the development of governments in their pristine state. In doing so he did not look any farther than an abstract type of procedure used by reasonable men to settle quarrels. He concluded that

> the great and chief end . . . of men uniting into commonwealths, and putting themselves under government, is the preservation of their property; to which in the state of Nature there are many things wanting.
>
> Firstly, there wants an established, settled, known law. . . . Secondly, in the state of Nature there wants a known and undifferent judge, with authority to determine all differences according to the established law. . . . Thirdly, in the state of Nature there often wants power to back and support the sentence when right, and to give it due execution . . . it being only with an intention in every one the better to preserve himself, his liberty and property. . . .

With the colonies just freed from the English Crown and with the necessity of forming a government for the protection of property rights, Locke's theory was the answer to the many questions facing the founding fathers. Consequently, they devised the documents of the new government to conform to Locke's theory of government, claiming a natural right of freedom for the individual as justification for their own overthrow of established authority.

The phraseology of the Declaration of Independence is Lockean from start to finish:

> We hold these truths to be self-evident, that all men are created equal; that they are endowed by their Creator with certain inalienable rights; that among these are life, liberty and the pursuit of happiness. That, to secure these rights, governments are instituted among men, deriving their just powers from the consent of the governed.

The "pursuit of happiness" of the Declaration was later changed to "property" in the Amendments to the Constitution, bringing that document in line with Locke's reasoning.

Shortly after the new government was established, there was considerable tension between the new federal government and the states. To clarify the position of the states, the Tenth Amendment was added to the Constitution. It in particular upholds the contracting theory of government providing a basis for states and individual rights against the federal government. The Tenth Amendment states that all powers not delegated to the United States by the Constitution nor prohibited by it to the states, are reserved to the states or the people. This means that certain powers which the individual held while in a state of nature have been surrendered by the people to their government on a contractual basis. Those powers not specifically surrendered that are inherent in the concept of individual rights remain with the individual person.

Lessons from the European past were not lost by the colonists who had fought the Revolution. Obvious and arbitrary abuse of sovereign powers and indiscriminate attacks on individuals made it imperative that the new government should not be given more authority than would be necessary to maintain order and protect itself against outside aggression. Among the new protections for individuals which the Constitution guaranteed were the prohibition against Bills of Attainder, so that no legislation specifically against individuals could be passed; a prohibition against ex post facto laws, so that no one could be punished because an act of his was later made criminal; a refusal to grant titles of nobility, to guard against the creation of a favored class; and the guarantee of the sanctity of contracts, to ensure stability in commercial transactions. Trials for treason were forbidden, except where the testimony of two witnesses could be introduced.

In the two centuries since the founding of the Republic, the concept of individual rights and protections has been greatly expanded. Particularly in the last decade, the Constitutional rights of those confronted by a criminal charge have been increased and defined so that today the United States has the best legal procedures in the world for the protection of individual citizens. Recent Supreme Court decisions such as *Gideon*, *Miranda*, and *Escobedo*, all dealing with the right to legal counsel, have provided an umbrella of protection for every citizen. Following the development of the protection of individual rights over the two centuries of American history, one only wonders why it took so long to articulate these principles. Rather than being a symptom of internal conspiracy, these cases stand for a high sense of individual worth and a lofty sense of justice.

Yet during the past several decades there has been an increasing sense of alienation felt by individuals, even while their legal rights have been clarified and expanded. The fabric of American society appears to be tearing apart with increasing speed, so that the legal definitions of individual rights provide no comfort to individual people. The sense of alienation indicates that there is something missing in our society's understanding of itself. Bundy's assertion that there is a gulf between ideals of individual dignity and equal opportunity thus pinpoints the problem. It is our understanding of what the individual really is that is faulty, since we cannot bring individual people the equal opportunity guaranteed to them by the Constitution. This is particularly true with respect to racial minorities in American society.

The Constitution is built upon a theory of radical idealism of the individual. It defines everything in terms of the solitary person willingly assuming his responsibilities as a citizen and participating in the forms of government on the basis of his understanding of absolute and abstract justice. Unfortunately, the world has never been composed of this type of individual. As far back as we can go in European history this abstract notion of the individual dominates thought, yet we have never found a person who fulfills this category of existence.

Religious individualism probably goes back to the Lutheran revolt against Papal powers. As Europeans broke the religious monolith of Catholic religious structure, the idea of the individual alone before his God guided only by his conscience, characterized Protestant thought. The rich cult and ceremony of the ancient Christian tradition was stripped of its social context and a stark barren form of worship was used to comprehend the solitude of the individual in his religious life.

The solitary individual of religion became a rugged individual in the field of economics as the Protestant ethic was transposed into the field of commerce. Again no effort was made to see beyond the theoretical basis of individual ownership of capital. It was felt that given the opportunity to prosper men would naturally achieve great wealth and position if they applied themselves to the situation at hand. When the colonists arrived on these shores and found a continent untouched by industry and commerce, they immediately set to work to develop it for themselves. Thus the settlement of North America fitted in perfectly with the economic theory derived from Protestant theology. It was every man for himself, since it appeared that there could never be an end to the resources of the continent and a person had only to grasp the opportunity that presented itself.

While there was theoretical justification for individualism in every field, the very paths of development did not support the theory in practice. Settlers came to the continent and promptly began to reincarnate their European heritage on a nationalistic basis. National groups created New York, New London, New Jersey, New Sweden, New France, New Spain, in an effort to settle specific areas on the basis of familiar patterns of life. The framers of the Constitution may have talked about the individual in abstract terms, but the pattern of settlement indicates that groupings according to nationality had more practical impact. While the Constitution spoke of one kind of government, actual settlement created another kind.

The new government was immediately plagued with two problems—land acquisition and slavery. Without land it could not push west to develop itself, and without cheap labor in the South it could not settle the country. The Constitution, although based upon the freedom and equality of all mankind, did not extend those rights to every group. The social compact was created among Western Europeans and it spoke only tangentially of non-Europeans. Congress was given authority to deal with the original inhabitants on the basis of regulating commerce. In the Interstate Commerce Clause, Indian tribes occupied a prominent position, and this was defined as a trade relationship between the United States and the various tribes of Indians.

Recognizing that the House of Representatives had to be composed of men elected on the basis of population, the compromise was reached that all black slaves were to be counted as three-fifths of a man for purposes of determining representation. After the Civil War, the phrase was changed by the civil rights amendments to count blacks on an equal basis.

Settlement of the country brought the American government into conflict with Mexico as people moved westward into Texas and the Southwest. After the annexation of the Texas Republic, the United States completed its conquest of the continent in the Mexican War and received the entire southwestern part of the United States in the Treaty of Guadalupe Hidalgo in 1848. Many Mexican citizens preferred to remain in the ceded area, so that in conquering the southwest territory the United States was forced to incorporate a substantial number of people who had a completely different political and social outlook from that of American citizens.

For the first hundred years, then, American society was dominated by people of Western European descent who accepted without question the political philosophy of John Locke buttressed by Protestant religious doctrines of individual salvation. The political system worked because all settlers from the Old World came to these shores as individuals, and they could affirm or deny their allegiance to the Constitution on the basis of individual choice. At the end of the first century, it had become apparent that slavery was irreconcilable with the ideology of the Constitution. It was inevitable that the question of slavery be resolved in order that the declaration of the equality of all men be realized. The Civil War was fought to define the meaning of the word "men" in the Constitution.

In 1848, Mexicans were brought into the Constitutional framework. In 1865 blacks were brought into the Constitutional framework, and in 1871, with the end of the treaty-making period,

Indian tribes were brought into the Constitutional framework. These compose the major racial minority groups today. It is important to note that IN NO CASE DID THESE GROUPS ENTER THE CONSTITUTIONAL FRAMEWORK AS INDIVIDUALS. Each group was given the franchise as a group. When McGeorge Bundy and other statesmen speak of the gulf between equal opportunity and individual worth they are grappling with this issue. We have seen over the past century the utter inability of American society to absorb these groups.

Entering the Constitutional framework as groups, Indians, blacks, and Mexicans have had to have legislative adjustments on their behalf every time they had a problem. In 1858 there was legislation to settle the claims of Mexican citizens stemming from the Treaty of Guadalupe Hidalgo. There has been a continual effort on the part of the black community to define its rights under this system of government. Thus we have had all manner of civil rights bills passed over the last century in an effort to provide equal opportunity to black citizens even though the Constitution provides for equality of opportunity. In many cases the wording of the legislation was significant, giving "all persons" the same rights as "white citizens." There have been some six thousand statutes passed concerning the rights and status of Indian tribes and individuals.

It has proven impossible to reconcile the desires of the three basic minority groups with the ideology of the Constitution that orients all considerations to protect the property-holding white citizen. Legislation concerning the three groups always revolves around property considerations. Thus Indian legislation designed to "free" the Indian individual always tampers with his rights to hold property in the tribal estate rather than as an individual. Civil rights bills are held up because they may perchance interfere with little Mrs. Murphy's right to run a boarding-house, Mr.

Maddox' right to sell chicken dinners to white folks, or a state's right to set the voting franchise on the basis of poll or property taxes.

The confusion of the past decade resulted from the fact that the civil rights movement broadened itself from simple economic integration and individualism to encompass the demands of the black group to determine its own destiny by developing power for itself in local communities. Voting rights and housing laws only served to emphasize the contention that American citizenship meant free and undisturbed use of public facilities and citizenship rights for a specific group. In a mere decade from 1954 to 1964 American society covered a century of time in defining what the word "citizen" meant. Then the civil rights movement shifted into group rights with the rise of Black Power.

We are now in the midst of the third ideological American revolution. It is a struggle to define the phrase "we the people." What is needed is not the rewriting of the Constitution but the recognition by society as a whole that there is a place in the Constitutional framework for group aspirations considered without reference to individualism. On a Lockean basis "we the people" means simply those people who happened to band together to provide law, order, and protection of property. On that criteria the Nixon Administration is absolutely correct in its return to strict Constitutional interpretation, and the continual effort to appoint men to the Supreme Court who will downgrade the rights of blacks and other minority groups stands squarely within the original ideology of the Constitution.

"We the people" in the contractual sense of the Constitution was written in a day when there was no recognition of minority groups. It was supported by the melting-pot ideology in which miscellaneous groups were expected to melt away into a mythical land of brotherhood. The social and cultural basis of "peoplehood" in this framework is Anglo-Saxon feudalism. We have never had a "peoplehood" in this country because we have always been tied to a barren conception of man. Where it is valid for individual men to contract with each other to provide certain services, the problem becomes very complicated when whole groups of people enter the situation.

Contracts can be made between individuals, even corporate individuals representing thousands of workers and administrators, since the corporate body is regarded as a single entity legally. But when groups of people are thrust into a political relationship, then it is impossible to use a contract basis. The situation clearly calls for a treaty or covenant relationship, since it encompasses the spirit of groups and not the behavior of individuals. Contracts have specific items which are severable, that is to say, can be fulfilled by themselves. Breaking a contract alters the relationship between men but cannot ultimately affect the relationships between groups of men.

The treaty-covenant relationship defines the spirit in which groups or nations will relate to one another. Little has to be spelled out in specific items because what is important is the pledge of faith between groups and the promise of each group to police itself on a moral basis. The disillusionment felt by members of the black community when passage of civil rights bills failed to bring any noticeable improvement in their condition, highlights the differences between white America and the minority groups. Minority groups have really been seeking a covenant-type pledge of faith from white society. White society has continued to pledge specific contractual rights to cure social ills. The gap of which Bundy and others are aware is between the aspirations of minority groups on the one hand and the individualistic idealism of white America on the other.

Taken together, all of the power movements and the emergence of the Woodstock Nation call for a renovation of state and federal laws on the basis of understanding the rights of groupings of people who have desires over and above the simple articulation of their individual rights. Thus the concept of "reparations" has recently come into existence in the black community. There is no simple answer for this demand since it speaks of payments due to the black community and not to any specific individual black for a specific wrong suffered. The rise and movement of the Alianza Federal de los Pueblos Libres, the Mexican group led by Reies Tijerina seeking a settlement of Mexican land claims in the Southwest, also highlights the problem of group rights.

In this sense, Constitutional recognition of the rights of groups, Indian tribes are much further ahead than are other groups. In 1946 the Indian Claims Commission was established to litigate outstanding claims that Indian tribes might have against the United States based on treaties and land cessions. This commission thus provides a prototype of structure by which the aspirations and claims of minority groups can be realized. Since the original conception of property rights for blacks advocated land and money as reparations and the Mexicans were guaranteed protection of their lands in the Southwest, it would seem that the crucial task ahead is to bring forward all property claims by minority groups for present settlement. This would mean a recognition by everyone concerned that the minority groups are at least even with white America as to property rights as we begin the third century of existence under the Constitution.

The problem is much more complex, however, than a simple recognition of property rights. The last few years have shown a motiveless militancy striking out against the governmental framework. Individuals have felt no sense of allegiance to federal or state governments because they have been deprived of their rights in the past and can feel no sense of urgency or justice in the present situation. There has not been a place in the governmental structure where mediation could take place. No recognition of the special interests and problems of groups has been made. Yet groups exist, as they always have, and people are excluded and discriminated against because of their membership in groups, whether racial, ethnic, or age groups.

Because it is difficult to vest individual loyalty in the Constitution, it has been felt that revising the Constitution would make it more feasible to deal with the gap between ideals and reality. There is a shorter and better method of revitalizing Constitutional beliefs and doctrines. Creation of new organizations at the local level would vest individual interests in supporting those institutions. Then, creating a special place within the Constitutional framework, would give the individual a special interest in defending the Constitutional form of government lest his own local institutions be endangered.

This is basic conservative political philosophy, but it has never been put into effect by conservatives. Instead, they have contented themselves with repeating the traditional phrases that appear to guarantee rights to individuals and local governments. States' rights is only a halfway house of rigorous conservative ideology and shows a reluctance to follow the obvious line of reasoning. If the federal government is too large and too active, then it should naturally follow with the complex society of today that states are also too large and interfering to vest ultimate powers of government in them. Bringing the issue down to the local level means that the local organization must reflect not simply the political rights of local people, but their culture, social system, economic resources and problems, and racial composition. The federal Constitution thus becomes the definition of ground rules for the interaction of group relationships.

The contemporary Indian tribe is a good illustration of how this principle can work. While individual Indians may complain bitterly against being ruled from long distance by a group of less-than-sympathetic whites, there has been no corresponding call for revolution and destruction of the present governmental scheme by Indian people. Indeed, the major complaints have been that the United States has failed to protect treaty rights of the tribes and that individual Indians have suffered accordingly. Indian tribes have a vested interest in maintaining the Constitutional framework, because tribal rights derive from this document and individuals receive from tribal rights the identity and status they seek as individuals.

When we view the contemporary social movements as forces breaking through simple individualism toward a broader conception of rights and recognition of specific groups, it becomes apparent that the revolutionary rhetoric used by militants today is the very antithesis of power and self-determination. Instead of advancing the philosophy of group rights as an alternative to Constitutional individualism, the militants seek the type of chaotic individualism that the Constitution was designed to prevent. They seek justice without order, which is impossible unless there is some attempt to define specific rights as a status guaranteed by the form of government established.

Militants have forced the defense of Anglo-Saxon individualism by the white community at a time when that principle was breaking apart and reforming along ethnic and group lines. Backlash has been channeled into a desire to return to the simplistic days of yore when the Constitution was written, a time when blacks, Mexicans, Indians, and youth were not considered able to form the social compact because they were separate groups. The call for revolution stands wholly within American tradition, but it speaks merely of renewing the ancient individualism which is rejected today by the very groups that call for revolution.

Unconsciously, American society has been moving toward other definitions of society and government. In providing for development of natural resources, various regional commissions have been set up. These provide for specific development of certain areas and peoples. The Tennessee Valley Authority, Missouri Valley Authority, the concern for Appalachia, the development of the Four Corners Area of Colorado, New Mexico, Arizona, and Utah all speak of forming local and regional governments on a supra-individual basis. Designation of development areas by the Economic Development Administration follows poverty lines rather than strict governmental organization built upon citizen-contracting theories.

With this trend already well developed, it remains for American society only to recognize group rights on the basis of race and culture to provide a thorough-going ideological revision of Constitutional theory to encompass modern problems. Thus the importance of Indian tribes today is the fact that they have managed to develop an extragovernmental status in the legal framework that, as the Supreme Court said in its decision of *Native American Church* v. *Navajo Tribe*, is "higher than states." With this additional status, racial minorities would be able to develop their rights on a suprastate basis, which is what the respective civil rights bills have done anyway by placing rights of black citizens on a federal basis, and eliminate much of the tension that exists between racial groups in contemporary society.

The contemporary interpretation of "we the people" in reality means "we the peoples," we the definable groups, and thus admits minority groups into Constitutional protection which they should have received as groups a century ago. This is the first and vital step in thinking that must be made if we are to continue on as a society until we have developed and understood the basis upon which we can be a varied people, inhabiting one nation with laws that can be used to fulfill all expectations of the cultural, social, economic, and religious nature of man in his own group. To continue merely on the basis of an abstract individual contracting with other individuals would be to court disaster.

9 * THE NEW ORGANIZATION

We have traditionally organized people and resources in two basic forms: profit-making corporations and nonprofit organizations. The accumulation of capital, development of income, and distribution of profits characterizes the profit-making corporations. To achieve this goal, land and natural resources have been destroyed, communities dispersed or dominated, and social problems unwittingly created. The profit-making corporations have generally disclaimed any responsibility for the conditions created by their activities.

The key to the profit-making corporation has been its recognition in law as an artificial person. Economic competition in our society has been a jungle inhabited by a multitude of artificial corporate persons competing against one another with the avowed intent of devouring the weaker species. Profit has determined survival, and other considerations have been cast aside in favor of success on the balance sheets. While corporations initially employed a number of people as wage-earners, thus providing employment for a substantial number of people, the trend has been one of continually searching for more efficient means of producing commercial goods. This trend has been publicized as providing a higher standard of living for all people, but it has in fact been a process of replacing men with machines. The result has been that a substantial number of people have been made obsolete by advanced technology.

Government has attempted to correct this situation by devising rules and regulations to curb extreme behavior of corporate individuals. The Full Employment Act of 1946 was passed specifically to recognize the right of individual people to have an income-producing job in spite of the increasing trend toward mechanization. In many areas, such as quality of products, level of prices, and distribution of goods, government regulations have meant practical elimination of the competitive spirit and uniformity of production by profit-making corporations. Where corporations have grouped together to fix prices or corner certain markets, laws have been used to keep corporations from completely dominating society.

The nonprofit alternative has been the opposite. Sensing that a large number of people, particularly minority groups and physically handicapped people, were being made victims of the economic warfare between corporate individuals, the nonprofit organization was devised to provide some refuge for the survivors of the economic wars. The nonprofit organization is not competitive in the economic field and therefore does not pay its entry fee (income tax) to enter the lists. It depends upon the largess of the profit-makers, corporate and individual, for its income and program. Neither entity, profit-making or profit-consuming, provides a useful vehicle for solution of social problems.

Society is polarized between organizations that produce income but have no social responsibility, and organizations that have no income but are designed to assume social responsibilities. People are either productive wage-earners or consumers incapable of producing income—but always in their individual capacity. Both poles of the equation have transient constituencies, since a person may move from one category to the other according to his economic fortunes.

This polarization has created the need for new organizational forms which are able to encompass both theories, and in which factors other than income can predominate. Cooperatives, credit unions, unions, and fraternal lodges have arisen to respond to this need. A great variety of socio-economic organizations now fill the gap between profit and nonprofit organizations. In recent years these organizations have been characterized by a rise in salaries and overhead to become competitive with private industry. They have additionally undertaken to solve difficult problems with political and economic overtones, so that the distinction between them and the ordinary commercial corporation is rapidly blurring. Tax-exempt nonprofit status now disguises movements of significant stature that are only casually related to the original charitable and educational goals.

Commercial corporations have also moved from their original profit-motive status. The major industries receive heavy subsidization from the federal government in a number of ways. Fringe benefits have been created for employees, and in some cases pension funds set aside for workers have purchased controlling stock in large corporations, in effect completing the circle and placing ownership of the corporation in the hands of the workers. Some corporations have undertaken training and placement programs for unemployed people as a means of recognizing their social duties. In effect, the old profit-oriented corporations have largely become social, semipublic entities.

While the two forms of organization have steadily moved

toward one another in their social roles, partisans of the old ideologies have reacted violently toward this change. Reactionary conservatives have denounced nonprofit organizations that serve specific purposes as Communist strongholds working to destroy the American way of life. Thus the NAACP, ACLU, and other well-known groups have been the targets of right-wing ire. New Left militants, on the other hand, have blasted the military-industrial complex in no uncertain terms. They credit it with achievements that it could not possibly bring about if it mustered all its resources and embarked on that course. Militants call for the disruption, and in some cases destruction, of industrial technology as a solution to social problems.

Unless the changing role of both types of organizations is recognized, the demand that both species be eliminated will continue to grow. The result will be either severe oppression by the right or destruction of the economic system by the left. Extremists of both stripes have been unwilling to try to bridge the ideological gap by the creation of a new type of social organization. Both sides speak of power, but few on either side understand its full implications and characterize it either as an economic weapon or an intangible wave of emotion.

By merging the present roles of profit and nonprofit organizations, we can understand that a profit-making corporation that expends its profits on social services for a distinct membership is the most useful vehicle for social change and organization. The entity would be productive in an economic sense, yet carry its profits to fulfill a responsible role in stabilizing society. By acknowledging and serving its immediate local society, it would be able to reduce expenditures now made for social services while maintaining economic independence.

There are two proposed types of organization that can fulfill this requirement: the Indian tribe and the Community Development Corporation as proposed by the Congress of Racial Equality. Indian tribes hold vast resources in tribal hands and with the income derived from tribal assets they serve the reservation communities. Since almost all tribal income goes to support tribal programs, the actual tax paid by Indian individuals is 100 percent of their interest in tribal property. Yet the programs of the tribe contribute to their ability to upgrade themselves economically, thus ensuring a type of social security system that covers every conceivable situation.

The tribe operates as a community of individuals in its elective processes. Its main concern is the ongoing life of the community, and thus it has an undifferentiated view of its economic-social-political-religious problems. Before termination of the Menominee Tribe of Wisconsin, the tribal sawmill was operated to provide employment for the reservation residents. Use of the major asset of the community to solve the major problem of the individual Indian has been a characteristic of tribal operations. Whenever the tribe enters into legal relationships with those outside the tribal community, it does so as a corporate person, thus ensuring a unity of purpose and posture toward the outside world. Tribes thus are able to incorporate the two extremes of traditional social and economic thought into one entity.

The Community Development Corporation advocated by CORE is another possibility for bridging the profit-nonprofit gap of today. The legislation authorizing the development of Community Development Corporations has yet to pass Congress, but developments in various places in the nation indicate the great need for the creation of this type of vehicle. Its basic thrust is to recognize the desires of local people to have a voice in decisions affecting them.

More specific information concerning the Community Development Corporation can be obtained from the Congress of Racial

Equality. The important thing to note is that the entire concept has a number of important aspects that would serve to greatly reduce the tensions that exist between various groups in American society. Unless we find other means of bridging the gaps that exist in society, the continued confusion and isolation will create an intolerable situation in which men may well resort to uncontrolled violence as a means of solving their problems. We have already seen individuals casually take rifles, sit on hillsides, and indiscriminately shoot at moving cars on freeways. Their situation is apparent. The modern universe has become so unreal to them that they are abstracted out of the real world and begin to regard it as a destructible toy. Then they simply destroy it because it is there.

The Community Development Corporation places the voting franchise at the age of sixteen and anyone in a local area to be served by a community corporation is eligible to vote to determine its policies and programs. This provision bridges the generation gap in the local communities in a much more realistic manner than society has tried to do with its national voting franchise. The trend recently has been to make special overtures to youth by setting up committees, commissions, advisory councils, and task forces to determine what place young people should have in American society. In doing this, young people are placed in a special category of semicompetency, for they are old enough to die for their country but not old enough to make any decisions regarding its government. Without a vested interest, they have been correct in advocating a radical change in status to jump from second-class robots to responsible citizens.

Setting up special committees has been another characteristic of government's attempts to discover the causes of violence and disorder in society. Two special committees have found that racism and propensity toward violence are hallmarks of American society. Each is characterized by a sense of alienation toward social values that are accepted by people in general. There is a continual feeling of solitude and the necessity to view survival as the most important aspect of life. Threats to any part of their traditional existence are manifested as backlash feelings toward minority races or tendencies to advocate violence as a solution to social problems.

If individuals feel helpless and threatened, a large part of their feeling of alienation may be because they are governed almost exclusively by a group of absentee administrators. Today, on all levels of government, we elect very few officials. In general, policies and programs are determined by people within the civil-service branches of government who remain in their jobs through every change of administration. Local communities have no recall provision on the majority of the people who are supposed to serve them. Policemen, teachers, firemen, garbage collectors, social welfare workers, and professional people do not necessarily live in the neighborhoods they serve. They therefore have no vested interest in correcting the specific ills of local neighborhoods, but are judged solely on the performance of their duties within the system in which they are employed.

With massive programs on the state and federal levels we have placed ourselves in the untenable position of being governed without our consent by people who really live in another kind of world. The whole sense of neighborhood has broken down so that each neighborhood takes on the aspect of a conquered country, overseen by a selected group of people who are arbitrarily placed in charge of the area to perform certain functions. Local people are not so much governed from Washington as they are governed by outsiders who are responsible to an abstract system of government that is determined by rules and regulations which generally do not apply to real problems of everyday life. The demand to eliminate federal services under the theory of a new federalism cannot solve the problems of the local neighborhood or small town, because it would simply be transferring the blame from one source to another without changing the means by which government relates to local people.

The genius of the Community Development Corporation is that it recognizes that all elected and appointed officials must be responsible to the people they are hired to serve. The CDC therefore has a residency requirement under which provisions only local people can be hired. The people who administer the programs are therefore subject to intangible community recall procedures because they have to work directly with the local people. A bureaucrat must account to local people after hours, informally, and continually since he must live in the neighborhood that he serves. It will be extremely difficult, therefore, for the programs to be abstracted from their practical setting in the community.

Another provision of the Community Self-Determination Act, which is the legislative package that would create the Community Development Corporation, is that a corporation could expand from its original area of service to provide services for a noncontiguous area. Policy-makers are continually divided on the question of development of rural areas. By and large the tendency has been to piously support the family farm as the last vehicle of rugged individualism and to pay lip service to industrial development of rural or remote areas. Yet the capital needs of rural areas are so great that it appears impossible for any government programs to begin to meet them.

What the Community Development Corporation is designed to do is to center itself in urban areas, build up capital, and then have the ability to branch out into noncontiguous areas, rural and remote, with sufficient capital to support development in those areas. With the migration already running heavy from rural to urban areas, this device would be the only means in the private area of resettlement of rural areas and balancing the tide of population concentration.

One of the problems that the Community Development Corporation has had is that it has been tied into the idea of black capitalism, which has been misinterpreted and ridiculed. The AFL-CIO, for example, termed black capitalism a "dangerous, divisive delusion offered as a panacea by extremists, both black and white, some businessmen who see a chance for profit and a few well-intentioned but misguided liberals." Part of the basic fear of the AFL-CIO was that the concept would be used to justify the establishment of sweatshops to prey on black workers without returning them to any state of economic advancement.

Newspaper editorials have also counseled against developing black capital, and some have stated that the only way to accumulate capital today is to marry into it. Other writers have emphasized the impossibility today of developing small businesses that are almost immediately swallowed up by chain stores and conglomerates. Some members of the press and labor councils have found black capitalism to be "apartheid anti-democratic nonsense." James Farmer, former head of the Congress of Racial Equality, and an Assistant Secretary for Administration in the Department of Health, Education and Welfare, in a speech in August, 1969, wanted to drop the entire label of black capitalism, since he said that "it seems to imply that our objective is to create just a few additional black millionaires, and that would not necessarily help the black community. It should include community corporations and cooperatives as well as private entrepeneurship."

The response of the Nixon Administration has thus far been nonexistent, either with respect to passage of the Community Self-Determination Act, which sets up the Community Development Corporations, or to the creation via the Small Business Administration of black capitalism. Campaign promises implied that additional credit guarantees would be used to support small businesses in the poverty-stricken communities, but outside of a small meeting in March, 1969, at the White House, little has been done to redeem the pledge of support.

The problem with community development is that it has been framed in traditional economic terms that do not take into account the obvious groupings along racial and ethnic lines that are the most significant movements of today. People have been thinking along economic lines that have been obsolete for hundreds of years. No effort has been made to relate nationalistic trends in the nation to economic needs of particular communities. Development schemes have been abstracted from the local setting into theoretical settings where they appear merely as principles of interpretation.

Reading deeply into the ideology of the Community Development Corporation one discovers that it is intended to create a "nation within a nation." This means not only totality of outlook, but a desperate need for community-owned capital. It is possible to see this need in the actual uses to which James Forman intended to put his reparations money. The Black Manifesto was a call for investment capital in land, publishing, education, and culture. It was fully in line with nationalistic uprisings in other groups, although its mode of presentation was different.

Understanding development on a nationalistic basis means that problems of police brutality, transportation, social services, education, welfare, and employment become problems internal to each national group. Because each group would be dependent upon a recognition of its rights of self-government by state and federal government, the self-policing aspect of nationalism would be very strong, eliminating many problems that exist today.

In several cities the idea of a police force responsible primarily to a group of people has already arisen. The Afro-American Patrolmen's League of Chicago is a good example of this trend. This organization acts to prevent injustice to members of the black community when they are threatened by white policemen. The National Society of Afro-American Policemen, with headquarters in New York City and chapters in Detroit, Newark, and Philadelphia, indicates a national concern by blacks for a more basic form of justice for their people. It also shows a concern by the black community for developing their own forms of law and order to fit the culture of their people.

During the rioting following the death of Martin Luther King, Jr., those cities in which the Black Panthers and other militant organizations had influence avoided violence and disorder. Cities where the black nationalists were without influence were hit hard. In 1967, black youths in Tampa, Florida, played a creative role in calming tempers during disturbances there. Saginaw and Grand Rapids, Michigan, have received grants from the Office of Economic Opportunity to fund youth patrols with excellent success in their programs. Boston has its Youth Alliance Security Patrol, also founded in 1967, which has proved so successful that the organization has branched out into job-placement programs and recreational activities. The result of these various programs has been the advocation by the Lemberg Center for the Study of Violence of the organization of youth patrols of young blacks to police their own neighborhoods and keep order.

This situation also applies to other groups. In Minneapolis, the American Indian Movement, AIM, established an Indian Patrol to check on reports of drunkenness among Indians of the Twin Cities. Prior to the organization of the patrol, the jails were filled every weekend with Indians on charges of drunk and disorderly. After thirty-eight weeks of Indian patrol work, the incidence of drunkenness was reduced to practically zero. This indicates that different norms and patterns of behavior apply to different groups. Where white policemen in Minneapolis always automatically arrested Indians who had been drinking and looting, whites in the same condition went safely home. Introduction of the Indian Patrol to ensure equal treatment for Indians reduced the problem to practically nothing.

The key, therefore, to the demand for "law and order" by white society would appear to be the cession of police powers and responsibilities to local groups, particularly in communities having a heavy concentration of ethnic and racial minority peoples. In like manner, full control over social welfare programs and resources by local communities would result in a better use of funds and more effective programs. At present, welfare programs are designed to meet external standards which do not correspond to conditions within American society. Welfare perpetuates dependency upon a distant bureaucracy with no corresponding sense of responsibility to the source of support.

Indian tribes requested control over welfare programs in 1966, when the Commissioner of Indian Affairs toured Indian country attempting to get the tribes' opinion on the state of Indian programs. Several tribes in the plains objected to the continual dole of welfare to their reservation people. In place of welfare checks, they proposed that all welfare funds come to the tribe for programming. Each tribe would create a number of programs to educate unemployed and handicapped people so that they would receive support for their participation in training programs and not simply for their inability to support themselves. The tribes suggested that ADC mothers be trained in homemaking skills and have a nursery to care for their children while in training. By learning food preparation, child care, budgeting, and sewing they would be better able to handle their immediate situation.

The proposal was turned down for a number of reasons. Liberals declared that no one should have to work for his welfare check, that it was his right under the Constitution to receive support from society. As an abstract principle of theory they were correct, but as a practical means of solving the problem of idleness and inability to maintain a home, their theory never spoke to the immediate problem at hand.

With the Community Development Corporation able to buy property in common for all its stockholders, the question of land and identity becomes important. In January, 1969, Floyd McKissick announced the effort to build a predominantly black city in a rural area in North Carolina. He had pledges from four industries to settle in the town and urban specialists from a number of prestige universities gathered to assist in the project. But the most important thing was McKissick's statement that "the black man has been searching for his identity and destiny in the cities. He should be able to find it on the plains of Warren County [North Carolina]." If McKissick had a useful vehicle like the Community Development Corporation, he would be able to fund Soul City by direct investment from the urban areas. It is this aspect of the proposal that has the most potential for the future.

Traditionally, gangs of youth have held sway over certain areas in the cities and terrorized neighborhoods. Control of crime in urban areas has always had an overtone of control of youth. Thus many neighborhoods have been polarized between young people and police, causing dissension and disruption. Recently some young gangs have gone beyond petty crimes and intergang warfare. They have adopted the corporate device as a means of perpetuating their influence on neighborhoods for constructive purposes. The Conservative Vice Lords, a Chicago gang of note, now owns and operates a malt shop, two pool halls, an agency that provides a security guard service to black-owned construction companies, an employment referral service, an art gallery and school, a tenant's union, and a crafts shop.

The Conservative Vice Lords have now started neighborhood cleaning and beautification programs. They are increasingly responding to other community needs, and it may well be that they have become the first post-riot corporation-social-service agency of this generation. Rather than go through the laborious task of developing a traditional profit-making corporation, the Vice Lords have remained nonprofit and have plowed their earnings back into further development projects.

Even white society has been using new corporate devices to solve social problems. Urban development is scheduled for Chicago's Skid Row. This project would ordinarily displace the hundreds of men who inhabit such areas, seeking an escape from the outside world. Care has been taken to develop a center for those men who do not wish to leave the neighborhood or return to their former place in society. This organizational device may prove very important in the future as a means of keeping communities intact, even though their surroundings are rebuilt.

With the many developments, both rural and urban, showing signs of creating a new status for organizations that desire to create profits which can be spent on providing ordinary social services, it may be time to take a new look at the way we have traditionally viewed our social problems. We have been taxing profit-making corporations, allowing a tax exemption for contributions to nonprofit organizations involved in social service and educational work. The tendency has been to split organizational distinctions on the basis of income and not on the basis of the relationships the organization has with its immediate community.

Tax-exempt organizations have now proliferated beyond counting, so that a great many agencies have been devised to cover the same area and population. Within the designated areas we have also found profit-making corporations that have had little impact on social services but which dominate the area economically. Thus we have built into our communities a wide gulf in roles and expectations, and have left ourselves without a viable alternative other than continued raising of taxes and creation of additional organizations to meet social needs.

The next logical step would appear to be the consolidation of tax-exempt organizations on a geographical or racial-ethnic basis, in preparation of the creation of Community Development Corporations which can serve specific areas and constituencies. As these groups are consolidated, the taxing power can be shifted to give exclusion from income tax for all amounts spent in social-service programs by profit and nonprofit organizations which engage in business activities. When Community Development Corporations have been established, nonprofit organizations would be required to withdraw from the fields in which CDCs were active, or merge with them to provide certain services. Profit-making corporations would be allowed to contribute as much money before taxes as they deem feasible. Then a high tax rate would be placed on their earnings, thus encouraging them to become more active members of their communities.

Gradual merging of the two basic organizational forms would give stability to neighborhoods, provide for local social services at the proper level, establish a resident administrative group, and eliminate the endless layers of bureaucracy. Each neighborhood would have to look at the totality of the world that confronted it, rather than attempt to solve problems on a piecemeal basis as is done at present. Public facilities shared by all people now would continue to be open to all persons making use of them. But in addition, there would be enclaves of racial, ethnic, urban, and rural groups that would have a sense of privacy and uniqueness untouched by the outside world. Alienation would be confined to those times that people stray from their own neighborhood into the worlds of other peoples. But everyone would have a homeland in which he had an important voice in determining the direction of his community.

There is really little alternative. The present scene is dominated by shoot-outs between Panthers and police. Large areas of urban settlements are being left vacant as neighborhoods deteriorate and buildings are abandoned by absentee apartment owners. The whole society shows signs of disintegrating in its universal aspect and reintegrating at the local level in new organizational structures. The Community Development Corporation is the new form of tribalism for people in the electric world. If nothing else, it allows time for people to regroup and determine their own lives. That would be enough to justify it if little else were ever accomplished.

10 * THE NEW INDIVIDUALISM

WE HAVE TWO antithetical ideas of the individual in today's society. One stems directly from the ideas held in the founding days of the Republic. At that time people assumed that a person, given free will and the right to exercise it, would generally make the correct decisions for himself and for his community. The voting franchise was thus considered to be the best method of arriving at a determination of the desires of the community at large, since any decisions made would be the result of the conscious and intelligent decisions of a number of responsible people.

This concept was more than optimistic. We have seen in practice that each person makes decisions according to his own good and hopes that somehow society will arrive at a wise and just decision in its deliberations. Unless a political movement is triggered by a charismatic political leader, society generally limps along postponing fundamental decisions because a majority of people want small adjustments and not major changes in their lives.

One theory of individualism has risen in recent years and is best characterized by the saying "do your thing." It indicates a complete freedom of movement for the individual person without regard to social goals and political movements. The remarkable thing is that the latter form of individualism has proven to be catalytic, whereas the more traditional understanding of the individual has produced stagnation and inability to comprehend mass movements.

Indians have always been the utmost individualists, but American society has failed to absorb them in its mainstream and there has been a continual warfare between the Indian tribes and the rest of society over this question. Yet the extreme individualism of the Indian has made it appear as if he would be suited above all to enter into the American social and political system. People are stunned to find that Indians totally reject American political ideology and concepts of equality, all the while being unable to reach any kind of conclusion within their own tribes as to programs and policies.

The vital difference between Indians in their individualism and the traditional individualism of Anglo-Saxon America is that the two understandings of man are built on entirely different premises. White America speaks of individualism on an economic basis. Indians speak of individualism on a social basis. While the rest of America is devoted to private property, Indians prefer to hold their lands in tribal estate, sharing the resources in common with each other. Where Americans conform to social norms of behavior and set up strata for social recognition, Indians have a free-flowing concept of social prestige that acts as a leveling device against the building of social pyramids.

Thus the two kinds of individualism are diametrically opposed to each other, and it would appear impossible to reconcile one with the other. Where the rich are admired in white society, they are not particularly welcome in Indian society. The success in economic wars is not nearly as important for Indians as it is for whites, since the sociability of individuals with each other acts as a binding tie in Indian society.

It is thus very important to understand the advent of the hippie and his subsequent influence on American life styles. The hippie, like the Indian, does not depend upon economic competition for his identity. He is more relaxed, more sociable, less worried about material goods, and more concerned with creating a community of others who share his interests and values. Youth of today fall into all grades of commitment to the new life style. Broadway shows reflect the new mode of life, books and magazines and underground newspapers chronicle it, and popular music spreads it abroad like a raging forest fire. Clothing and hair styles are creeping forward into age groups that formerly rejected out of hand a change in values.

The important thing about the hippie, and one thing that has certainly been missed by older commentators, is that the release from economic competition has created the necessity to derive a new identity based on other than economic criteria. Thus some of the most active and enthusiastic people in the new movement have been children of affluent homes that have not had to face economic competition. Born into the good life, they have been at a loss for identity since early childhood, and they have been the first generation that has been able to examine itself purely on the basis of feelings and experiences.

Older people have been horrified because their children have rejected out of hand the riches and power that they have spent so much time accumulating. They grew up in the Depression, where a lack of economic power meant relegation to a long line of unemployed, broken, status-less people. Thus the older generation promptly sought and in many cases achieved a position of economic power in which they could express their identity as a person without suffering the demeaning indignity of being another man in a long line or another number in an endless list of numbers.

The generation gap is more than an age difference in many ways. It reflects a difference in views of the world. The younger generation sees the world as inhabited by persons who must in some way relate to each other. The older generation understands the world as an economic jungle where, without allies, the individual is crushed by forces beyond his control. If the world of economic reality is destroyed, then the older generation will lose identities that it has struggled all its life to achieve. If there is continued economic definition of man, then the younger generation will feel hopelessly trapped with identities it does not accept or understand.

The ideological basis of society is thus shifting every year as the older generation dies off and the younger generation becomes more radical in its search for itself. Programs such as the Peace Corps, VISTA, and poverty projects are mildly regarded by older people as a means of expending excess energy of the younger generation until such time as they enter the economic wars. But these programs are looked at primarily in terms of experiences by younger people, so that service in one of these programs acts as a catalyst in determining life values, and only drives more people to reject an economic determination of their lives.

When competition becomes freed from its economic foundation, as it has been in the Indian tribes, then life takes on a whole new aspect. Status depends upon the manner in which a person contributes to his community. Knowledge for knowledge's sake becomes an irrelevant assertion, because it does not directly contribute to the elevation of people within the group. It becomes much more important that a person be wise and enter into the decisions of the group than that he know a great number of facts. Science is the handmaiden of economics because it creates tools by which men can climb the economic ladder, but it is useless in a noneconomic society because it is an abstraction of life.

Eliminating economic competition from a society thus creates a change of great dimensions. Wisdom with respect to the immediate situation is much more valuable than is the ability to consume and dispense great gobs of knowledge. Depth rather than breadth characterizes the tribal society. In the younger generation we can already see a rabid devouring of esoteric works in search of wisdom, and their poetry reflects a more sophisticated understanding of life than does the work of previous generations. Dylan's poetry, for example, caricatures the procedures by which the older generation operates, warning the youth that this is ephemeral and perhaps a charade that may fascinate but also entrap.

The outrageous clothing worn by young people emphasizes the "beautiful" aspect of their lives. It corresponds in many ways to Indian war-bonnet vanity and the desire to demonstrate acceptance by the group and honored status. It is no accident that many hippies wear beads and buckskin, because these combine simplicity of economic origin with advertisement of personal worth. Beads are extraneous to clothing, yet they become an integral part of personality.

The contemporary movement toward communes also emphasizes tribalistic life and is not competitive in economic terms. The concept of massing great stores of wealth runs counter to the demand that a person be respected in his group because of what he is. For that reason Charlie Manson's charisma was much more important than his ability to provide an economic base for his "family." As communes gather, the standard of living is defined by the group and not by outside forces. Thus communes can exist because they provide an understanding of togetherness which then defines economic reality. The older generation views it differently, feeling that economic considerations come first and neighborhoods form on that basis. Thus the suburbs are settled according to economic ability to provide and not sociability of people. Families are isolated in the suburbs because all they have in common is a bank balance of a certain size and the ability to keep it replenished.

While advocating education as the sure means of climbing the socio-economic ladder, education has been anything but individual-oriented. Children are hustled from grade to grade, whether they understand or not. Tests periodically separate the talented from the untalented and the winnowing process continues through college and graduate school. It is a simple case of running an intellectual obstacle course that keeps narrowing as the end approaches. The goal is to be certified for a job within the system. Any suggestion that the course could be covered in less time appears heretical and unworthy of consideration.

Because college and graduate schools are so costly, and because the poorer families do not have the funds to keep their children in school, education is merely an aspect of the economic system. Any particular child can be kept in the race only as long as there are funds to keep him running. When the money runs out or proves too little to continue the race, the child is finished, unless he can borrow or earn the money to remain in the competition. Recent studies have shown that children formerly considered ineligible for college have done about as well as children considered ready for college. What was needed was economic support for the college years, not additional training to prepare them for the great challenge.

When economic competition is seen in relation to land, the question becomes WHAT is the land used for, and not WHOSE land is it. There is consequently the tendency to regard land as a commodity for sale, and no attachment can be formed with the land. People buy and sell land as if it were another piece in a game of chess, rather than understanding that they have a relationship to it. Many pieces are bought and sold and never seen by the buyers and sellers. There is consequently no feeling of responsibility to keep the land fruitful, since it is recognized only to produce economic gain. Companies and individuals consume land for their own purposes without recognizing that they are depleting their own valued resources.

The tribal-communal way of life, devoid of economic competition, views land as the most vital part of man's existence. It is THEIRS. It supports them, tells them where they live, and defines for them HOW they live. Land does not have the simple sentimentality of purple mountains majesty or the artificial coloring of slides taken by tourists. It is more than a passing fancy to be visited on a vacation and forgotten. Rather it provides a center of the universe for the group that lives on it. As such, the people who hold land in this way always have a home to go to. Their identity is secure. They live with it and do not abstract themselves from it and live off it.

Economic competition in religious life defines denominations. Churches grade people and congregations according to income received. Sermons are tailored to fit the conceptions and beliefs held by the economic class to which they are addressed. The rise of a person economically often tells his life's theological journey, traveling from Baptist to Methodist to Presbyterian to Episcopalian as his fortunes rise. In some areas economic competition defines the very buildings in which religious services are held, with escalating wars between congregations and a corresponding rise in prices for electric organs, stained-glass windows, pews and pulpits, and fast-talking preachers.

Eliminating economic determination from religious life levels the whole structure of organized religion. There is no way to distinguish between the validity of religious beliefs except by experience. Thus spirituality defines religious constituencies, and not affluence and ostentatious display. God cannot be pleased or glorified by a $10,000 organ because he does not recognize the ability to purchase as a religious criterion. The drive of youth into esoteric religions, drugs, astrology, reincarnation, and mysticism only emphasizes the individualistic aspect of religion in a non-competitive manner. Gathering together for experiences, young people have the option of accepting or rejecting religious ideas on the basis of their own experiences rather than accepting authority outside themselves as the criteria for judgments.

The result of the new individualism is that groups are formed that have experiences in common. Status is gained according to personal recognition by others of the trueness of the individual. Consistency of viewpoint is the hallmark of the new individualism, yet the world view held by younger peoples is so comprehensive that it often appears contradictory to people of the older generation who think in rigid categories of interest.

The Woodstock Nation is thus the result of a feeling of humanity shared by a substantial number of people. In a sense it did represent a gathering of the tribes in the same way that the old Sioux nation, in the days before the white men came, met every year near Bear Butte in northwestern South Dakota, to visit, exchange presents, and renew the existence of the tribe. Many people have downgraded the youth because there have not been a series of Woodstocks each greater than the previous one. But this would degrade the very basis for meeting in concert.

Identity derived from economic status will probably be with us to some degree for a great while. It serves as a means of distinguishing between people and in turn promotes economic growth necessary to keep society operating. That is, it is not all bad and has proven useful to all Americans in a number of ways. The real problem is that we have passed the point of no return with respect to economics. Machines and computers are now so efficient that they are eliminating the ability and opportunity of most people to compete economically. Whether we like it or not we have undertaken to remove ourselves from the economic equation that was designed to support American society.

Already conservatives are talking about the guaranteed annual income, and the major part of American industry is on subsidy or economic existence guaranteed by government support. Without the ability or necessity to compete economically as a means of distinguishing between individuals, society must necessarily change to another form of identity-formation. This is what the younger generation has largely done and it happens to coincide with tribalistic forms already present in Indian tribes. Thus social movement, after four centuries of economic determinism, is reverting to pre-Columbian expressions, although modified by contemporary technology.

With machines producing an overabundance of wealth, the primary task of people will be to consume what is produced, lest the system break apart by overproduction. Agriculture already has broken apart, with large areas held out of production, and the result has been the breakdown of rural society. Suicides range higher in those rural areas where affluence and support appears to be greatest, because the people have not yet adjusted to the vacuum created by the absence of economic competition. Thus Iowa, one of the richest farm states, has had a consistently high suicide rate for a state with an apparently stable rural population.

We can look forward to a tremendous drive for social reform in spite of ourselves. Already graduates of prestige colleges and universities are going into social service programs instead of business. Public-interest law firms are on the increase. Free universities are rising everywhere. The separate disciplines of former days are being torn out of the institutions that entrapped them and thrust into the street. The university as the "marketplace of ideas" has become an absurdity, but off-campus the ideas flow with increasing vigor and insight. Even the conservation movement is gearing up to demand a reevaluation of land use for the benefit of all of society instead of the profit of a few people.

Whether we like it or not, the movement is steadily in one direction. The best that we can do is to open up as many options as possible so that the polarization of groups and group values does not freeze movements into violent confrontations. This would mean dropping traditional ideas and getting behind them to discover what we think we have been trying to do. Persecution of one group for smoking pot while another group destroys itself via nicotine and alcohol is a refusal to face reality. Subsidization of large farms while quibbling over pennies in food stamps is ridiculous. Authorizing supersonic transport planes while cutting education budgets is absurd.

In the field of education alone, radical changes could be made to open the present system up to the challenges presented by individuals. The twelve years of primary and secondary school has become a sacred cow that really defines the nature of babysitting more than it does education. We continually build more schoolhouses to "seat" so many children. We should be providing an escape hatch for those who are ready and able to go forward. If a student can read, absorb, and retain a certain amount of knowledge in a week, he should receive credit for that achievement and be able to move on. The present educational system looks the other way at students who skip classes, study hard for finals, and score high in tests. It traps a number of capable people in an endless round of classroom boredom under the pretense that mere attendance is equal to education.

By opening up social structures to rapid change, we will be allowing people to group themselves according to their interests and experiences. Formal recognition of groups will mean a coming-together of society on the realistic basis of self-interest. Each group will be incapable of overriding other groups on an economic basis, and to maintain its identity and cohesion it will have to have internal integrity. Individual people will have the right and motivation to flow through groupings on the basis of their own experiences and interests, and neighborhoods and communities will reflect a new kind of social reality that has been experienced as yet only during crises situations when everyone was thrown together in order to survive.

The "do-your-thing" doctrine of youth presents the ultimate challenge to American society, for it challenges society to expand its conception of the individual beyond the field of economics. It creates criteria by which a total sense of person and humanity can be defined. "Doing-your-thing" speaks of what a man IS, not what he HAS. In this type of change Indians are far ahead of the rest of society and may be steadily pulling away from the rest of the pack. Hence the absurdity of studies on how to bring Indians into the mainstream when the mainstream is coming to the tribe.

The change in ideology is important to recognize. It means that eventually the land upon which people lives determines how they will live. Before the coming of the white man the land was untouched. It provided for everyone and people dared not disturb it since it was the property of all. There was no need for industry or tedious work, since the land provided.

Over a period of four hundred years the white man has completely changed the land. But the land has not given up its powers. Today society is almost completely industrialized and the land is almost completely settled. Yet the wealth of natural resources and technological innovations have created a type of society in which it will not require tedious work and everyone will be forced to live in small tribal groups because that will be the only way to survive.

Thus whether the land is developed or not, and whether the people desire it or not, the land determines the forms by which societies are able to live on this continent. An undeveloped land created tribes and a fully developed land is creating tribes. In essence Indians have really won the battle for cultural survival. It remains only for years to go by and the rise of youth to continue, and everyone will be in the real mainstream of American life—the tribe.

11 * THE ARTIFICIAL UNIVERSE

THE JUSTIFICATION for taking lands from Indian people has always been that the needs and requirements of civilized people had to come first. Settlers arriving on these shores saw a virtual paradise untouched by the works of man. They drooled at the prospect of developing the land according to their own dictates. Thus a policy of genocide was advocated that would clear the land of the original inhabitants to make way for towns, cities, farms, factories, and highways. This was progress.

Even today Indian people hold their land at the sufferance of the non-Indian. The typical white attitude is that Indians can have land as long as whites have no use for it. When it becomes useful, then it naturally follows that the land must be taken by whites to put to a better use. I have often heard the remark "what happens to the Indian land base if we decide we need more land?" The fact that Indian rights to land are guaranteed by the Constitution of the United States, over four hundred treaties, and some six thousand statutes seems irrelevant to a people hungry for land and dedicated to law and order.

The major reason why whites have seen fit to steal Indian lands is that they feel that their method of using land is so much better than that of the Indian. It follows that God would want them to develop the land. During the Seneca fight against Kinzua Dam, sympathetic whites would raise the question of Indian legal rights and they would be shouted down by people who said that the Indians had had the land for two hundred years and did *nothing* with it. It would be far better, they argued, to let whites take the land and develop something on it.

From the days of the earliest treaties, Indians were shocked at the white man's attitude toward land. The tribal elders laughed contemptuously at the idea that a man could sell land. "Why not sell the air we breathe, the water we drink, the animals we hunt?" some replied. It was ludicrous to Indians that people would consider land as commodity that could be owned by one man. The land, they would answer, supports all life. It is given to all people. No one has a superior claim to exclusive use of land, much less does anyone have the right to fence off a portion and deny others its use.

In the closing decades of the last century, Indian tribes fought fiercely for their lands. Reservations were agreed upon and tribes held a fragment of the once expansive hunting grounds they had roamed. But no sooner had Indians settled on the reservations, than the government, ably led by the churches, decided that the reservation areas should be divided into tiny plots of land for farming purposes. In many reservation areas it was virtually impossible to farm such lands. The situation in California was so desperate that a report was issued denouncing the government land policy for Indians. The report contained such detrimental material exposing the vast land swindles that it was pigeonholed in the Senate files and *has never been released and cannot be obtained today, nearly a century later!!!*

Tribe after tribe succumbed to the allotment process. After the little plots of land were passed out to individual Indians, the remainder, which should have been held in tribal hands, was declared surplus and opened to settlement. Millions of "excess" acres of lands were thus casually transferred to federal title and given to non-Indian settlers. Churches rushed in and grabbed the choice allotments for their chapels and cemeteries, and in some cases simply for income-producing purposes. They had been the chief advocates of allotment—on the basis that creating greed and selfishness among the Indians was the first step in civilizing them and making them Christians.

For years the development of the land did make it seem as if the whites had been correct in their theory of land use. Cities were built, productive farms were created, the wilderness was made safe, and superhighways were built linking one portion of the nation with the others. In some areas the very landscape was changed as massive earth-moving machines relocated mountains and streams, filled valleys, and created lakes out of wandering streams.

Where Indian people had had a reverence for the productiveness of the land, whites wanted to make the land support their way of life whether it was suited to do so or not. Much of San Francisco Bay was filled in and whole areas of the city were built upon the new land. Swamps were drained in the Chicago area and large portions of the city were built on them. A great portion of Ohio had been swamp and grassland and this was drained and farmed. Land was the great capital asset for speculation. People purchased apparently worthless desert land in Arizona, only to have the cities grow outward to their doorstep, raising land prices hundreds of percents. Land worth pennies an acre in the 1930s became worth thousands of dollars a front foot in the 1960s.

The rapid increase of population, technology, and capital has produced the present situation where the struggle for land will surpass anything that can be conceived. We are now on the verge of incredible development of certain areas into strip cities that will extend hundreds of miles along the coasts, major rivers, and mountain ranges. At the same time, many areas of the country are steadily losing population. Advanced farming techniques allow one man to do the work that several others formerly did, so that the total population needed in agricultural states continues to decline without a corresponding decline in productivity.

The result of rapid industrialization has been the creation of innumerable problems. Farm surpluses have lowered prices on agricultural products so that the federal government has had to enter the marketplace and support prices to ensure an adequate income for farmers. Farm subsidies are no longer a small business. In nine wheat and feed grain-producing counties in eastern Colorado in 1968, $31.4 million was given in farm subsidies. In all of Colorado, $62.8 million was given in 1968 to support farmers. This was a state with a declining farm population. Under the Agricultural Stabilization Conservation Service, some $3.5 billion was paid out in 1968, $675 million paid to 33,395 individual farmers as farm "income maintenance," some receiving amounts in excess of $100,000.

For much of the rural farm areas the economy, the society, and the very structure of life is completely artificial. It depends wholly upon government welfare payments to landowners, a thinly disguised guaranteed annual income for the rich. If the payments were suddenly cut off, millions of acres would become idle because it would not pay to farm them and there would be no way to live on them without income. Our concern for the family farm and the rural areas is thus a desperate effort to maintain the facade of a happy, peace-loving nation of farmers, tillers of the soil who stand as the bastion of rugged individualism.

If rural areas have an artificial economy, the urban areas surpass them in everything. Wilderness transformed into city streets, subways, giant buildings, and factories resulted in the complete substitution of the real world for the artificial world of the urban man. Instead of woods, large buildings rose. Instead of paths, avenues were built. Instead of lakes and streams, sewers and fountains were created. In short, urban man lives in a world of his own making and not in the world that his ancestors first encountered.

Surrounded by an artificial universe where the warning signals are not the shape of the sky, the cry of the animals, the changing of seasons, but simply the flashing of the traffic light and the wail of the ambulance and police car, urban people have no idea what the natural universe is like. They are devoured by the goddess of progress, and progress is defined solely in terms of convenience within the artificial technological universe with which they are familiar. Technological progress totally defines the outlook of most of America, so that as long as newer buildings and fancier roads can be built, additional lighting and electric appliances can be sold, and conveniences for modern living can be created there is not the slightest indication that urban man realizes that his artificial universe is dependent on the real world.

Milk comes in cartons, and cows are so strange an animal that hunters from large cities kill a substantial number of cattle every year on their annual hunting orgies. This despite the fact that in many areas farmers paint the word COW on the side of their animals to identify them. Food comes in plastic containers highly tinged with artificial sweeteners, colors, and preservatives. The very conception of plants, growing seasons, rainfall, and drought is foreign to city people. Artificial criteria of comfort define everything that urban areas need and therefore dominate the producing rural areas as to commercial products.

The total result of this strange social order is that there has been total disregard for the natural world. The earth is considered simply another commodity used to support additional suburbs and superhighways. Plant and animal life are subject to destruction at the whim of industrial development. Rivers are no more than wasted space separating areas of the large cities. In many areas they are open sewers carrying off the millions of tons of refuge discarded by the urban consumer.

The Indian lived with his land. He feared to destroy it by changing its natural shape because he realized that it was more than a useful tool for exploitation. It sustained all life, and without other forms of life, man himself could not survive. People used to laugh at the Indian respect for smaller animals. Indians called them little brother. The Plains Indians appeased the buffalo after they had slain them for food. They well understood that without all life respecting itself and each other no society could indefinitely maintain itself. All of this understanding was ruthlessly wiped out to make room for the white man so that civilization could progress according to God's divine plan.

In recent years we have come to understand what progress is. It is the total replacement of nature by an artificial technology. Progress is the absolute destruction of the real world in favor of a technology that creates a comfortable way of life for a few fortunately situated people. Within our lifetime the difference between the Indian use of land and the white use of land will become crystal clear. The Indian lived with his land. *The white destroyed his land. He destroyed the planet earth.*

Non-Indians have recently come to realize that the natural

world supports the artificial world of which they are so fond. Destruction of nature will result in total extinction of the human race. There is a limit beyond which man cannot go in reorganizing the land to suit his own needs. Barry Commoner, Director of the Center for the Biology of Natural Systems at Washington University in St. Louis, has been adamant about the destruction of nature. He told a Senate Subcommittee on Intergovernmental Affairs that the present system of technology would destroy the natural capital, the land, air, water, and other resources within the next fifty years. He further pointed out that the massive use of inorganic fertilizers may increase crop yields for a time but inevitably changes the physical character of the soil and destroys the self-purifying capability of the rivers. Thus the rivers in Illinois have been almost totally destroyed, while the nitrate level of rivers in the Midwest and California has risen above the safe level for use as drinking water.

A conference on pollution in Brussels outlined the same problem and had a much earlier deadline in mind. Scientists there predicted the end of life on the planet within a minimum of thirty-five years. Elimination of the oxygen in the atmosphere was credited to jet engines, destruction of oxygen-producing forests, and fertilizers and pesticides such as DDT that destroy oxygen-producing microorganisms. Combining all of the factors that are eliminating the atmosphere, the scientists could not see any future for mankind. Realization of the situation is devastating.

Even where forests and plant life exist, the situation is critical. In southern California millions of trees are dying from polluted air. A recent aerial survey by the Forest Service in November, 1969, showed 161,000 acres of conifers already dead or dying in southern California. The situation has been critical since 1955, when residents of the area discovered trees turning yellow, but no one even bothered to inquire until 1962. In the San Bernardino forest 46,000 acres of pine are already dead and close to 120,000 acres more are nearly dead.

With strip cities being developed that will belch billions of tons of pollutants skyward every day the pace will rapidly increase so that optimistic projections of fifty to a hundred years more of life must be telescoped to account for the very rapid disappearance of plant life by geometrically increasing pollution. The struggle for use of land has polarized between conservationists, who understand that mankind will shortly become extinct, and developers, who continue to press for immediate short-term financial gains by land exploitation.

The Bureau of Land Management, alleged guardian of public lands, has recently been involved in several controversial incidents with regard to its policies. In one case Bureau officials reversed themselves and acceded to Governor Jack Williams' request to transfer 40,000 acres of federal range to the state "so the land could be leased to ranchers." Stewart Udall, the great conservationist, upheld the original decision of the Bureau of Land Management because he thought that federal lands closer to cities could be obtained for development purposes. The overall effect of government policies on land is to silently give the best lands to state or private development without regard for the conservation issue or the public welfare.

We can be relatively certain that the federal and state governments will not take an objective view of land use. Agencies established to protect the public interest are subject to heavy political pressure to allow land to slip away from their trusteeship for short-sighted gains by interest groups. This much is certain: at the moment there is not the slightest chance that mankind will survive the next half century. The American public is totally unconcerned about the destruction of the land base. It still believes in the infallibility of its science, technology, and government. Sporadic and symbolic efforts will receive great publicity as the future administrations carefully avoid the issue of land destruction. Indian people will find their lands under continual attack and will probably lose most of them because of the strongly held belief that progress is inevitable and good.

With the justification of progress supporting the destruction of Indian tribes and lands, the question of results becomes important. Four hundred years of lies, cheating, and genocide were necessary in order for American society to destroy the whole planet. The United States government is thus left without even the flimsiest excuse for what has happened to Indian people, since the net result of its machinations is to destroy the atmosphere, thus suffocating mankind.

There is a grim humor in the situation. People used to make fun of Indians because of their reverence for the different forms of life. In our lifetime we may very well revert to panicked superstition and piously worship the plankton of the sea, begging it to produce oxygen so that we can breathe. We may well initiate blood sacrifices to trees, searching for a way to make them productive again. In our lifetime, society as a whole will probably curse the day that white men landed on this continent, because it will all ultimately end in nothingness.

Meanwhile, American society could save itself by listening to tribal people. While this would take a radical reorientation of concepts and values, it would be well worth the effort. The land-use philosophy of Indians is so utterly simple that it seems stupid to repeat it: man must live with other forms of life on the land and not destroy it. The implications of this philosophy are very far-reaching for the contemporary political and economic system. Reorientation would mean that public interest, indeed the interest in the survival of humanity as a species, must take precedent over special economic interests. In some areas the present policies would have to be completely overturned, causing great political dislocations in the power structure.

In addition to cleaning up streams and rivers and cutting down on air pollution, a total change in land use should be instituted. Increase in oxygen-producing plants and organisms should be made first priority. In order to do this, vast land areas should be reforested and bays should be returned to their natural state. At present, millions of acres of land lie idle every year under the various farm programs. A great many more acres produce marginal farming communities. Erosion and destruction of topsoil by wind reduces effectiveness of conservation efforts. All of this must change drastically so that the life cycle will be restored.

Because this is a total social problem and the current solutions such as sporadic national and state parks and soil banks are inadequate answers, a land-use plan for the entire nation should be instituted. The government should repurchase all marginal farmlands and a substantial number of farms in remote areas. This land should be planted with its original growth, whether forest or grassland sod. The entire upper midwest plains area of the Dakotas and Montana and upper Wyoming should become open-plains range with title in public hands. Deer, buffalo, and antelope should gradually replace cattle as herd animals. Outside of the larger established towns, smaller towns should be merely residences for people employed to redevelop the area as a wilderness.

Creeks and streams should be cleared of mining wastes and their banks replanted with bushes and trees. The Missouri should be returned to its primitive condition, except where massive dams have already been built. These should remain primarily as power-generating sites without the corresponding increase in industry surrounding them. Mining and tourism should be cut to a minimum and eventually prohibited. The present population could well be employed in a total conservation effort to produce an immense grasslands filled with wildlife.

The concept is not impossible. Already a rancher in Colorado has tried the idea of grazing wild animals and beef cattle on his range with excellent results. Tom Lasater has a 26,000-acre ranch east of Colorado Springs, Colorado. He has pursued a no-shooting, no-poisoning, no-killing program for his land. There has already been a substantial increase in game animals, primarily mule deer and antelope, without any disturbance to his beef animals. Lasater first decided to allow wild animals to remain on his land when his foreman remarked, after the prairie dogs had been exterminated, that the grass always grew better when the prairie dogs had been allowed to live on the land.

The result of Lasater's allowing the land to return to its primitive state has been the notable decrease of weeds. Lasater feels that the smaller animals, such as gophers, ground squirrels, badgers, and prairie dogs, that dig holes all provided a better means of aerating the ground and introducing more oxygen into it than modern farming methods of periodically turning the sod by plowing. All of the wildlife use on the land produced better grazing land and reduced the danger of overgrazing in a remarkable way. The fantastic thing about Lasater's ranch is that it returns almost double the income from beef cattle, because of the improved conditions of the soil and the better grasses, than would the average ranch of comparable acreage using the so-called modern techniques of ranching.

The genius of returning the land to its original animals is that the whole program cuts down on labor costs, maintains fertility far better than modern techniques, increases environmental stability, and protects the soil from water and wind erosion. The net result is that the land supports much more life, wild and domestic, and is in better shape to continue to support life once the program is underway. Returning the major portion of the Great Plains to this type of program would be the first step in creating a livable continental environment. But introduction of this kind of program would mean dropping the political platitudes of the rancher and farmer as America's last rugged individualists, admitting that they are drinking high on the public trough through subsidies, and instituting a new kind of land use for the areas involved.

In the East and Far West, all land that is not immediately productive of agricultural products for the urban areas should be returned to forest. This would mean purchasing substantial acreage in Wisconsin, Ohio, Michigan, New York, New Jersey, and Pennsylvania and planting new forests. With the exception of settled urban areas, the remainder of those states would probably become vast woods as they were originally. Wildlife would be brought in to live on the land since it is an irreplaceable part of the forest ecology. With the exception of highspeed lanes for transportation facilities, the major land areas of the East Coast would become forest and woodlands. The presence of great areas of vegetation would give carbon-dioxide-consuming plants a chance to contribute to the elimination of smog and air pollution.

The social structure of the East would have to change considerably. In New York City the number of taxicabs is limited because unimpeded registration of cabs would produce a city so snarled with traffic that there would be no transportation. In the same manner anyone owning a farm of substantial acreage would have to be licensed by the state. The rest of the land would become wilderness with a wildlife cycle supporting the artificial universe of the cities by producing relatively clean air and water. The countless millions now on welfare in the eastern cities could be resettled outside the cities with conservation jobs and in retirement towns to ensure that the green belt of oxygen-producing plants would be stabilized.

In the coal mining states strip mining would be banned and a substantial number of people could be employed in work to return the land to its natural state. Additional people could harvest the game animals and the food supply would partially depend upon meat from wild animals instead of DDT-bearing beef animals. Mines would be filled in and vegetation planted where only ugly gashes in the earth now exist. People disenchanted with urban society would be allowed to live in the forests with a minimum of interference. Any who might want to live in small communities and exist on hunting and fishing economies would be permitted to do so.

On the seacoasts, pollution should be cut to a minimum. Where there are now gigantic ports for world shipping, these would be limited to a select few large enough to handle the trade. Others would have to become simply ports for pleasure boats and recreation. Some of the large commercial centers on both coasts would have to change their economy to take into account the absence of world trade and shipping. Beaches would have to be cleaned and set aside as wilderness areas or used by carefully selected people as living areas. Lobster beds, oyster beds, and areas that used to produce edible seafood would have to be returned to their original condition.

The pollution crisis presents the ultimate question on tribalism. If mankind is to survive until the end of the century, a substantial portion of America's land area must be returned to its original state of forest and grasslands. This is fundamentally because these plants produce oxygen and support the life cycle at the top of which is man. Without air to breathe it is ridiculous to speak of progress, culture, civilization, or technology. Machines may be able to live in the present environment, but it is becoming certain that people cannot.

By returning the land to its original state, society will have to acknowledge that it can no longer support two hundred million people at an artificial level of existence in an artificial universe of flashing lights and instantaneous communications. To survive, white society must return the land to the Indians in the sense that it restores the land to the condition it was in before the white man came. And then to support the population we now have on the land that will be available, a great number of people will have to return to the life of the hunter, living in the forests and hunting animals for food.

Whenever I broach this subject to whites, they cringe in horror at the mere prospect of such a development. They always seem to ask how anyone could consider returning to such a *savage and unhappy state*, as the government reports always describe Indian life. Yet there is a real question as to which kind of life is really more savage. Does the fact that one lives in a small community hunting and fishing for food really indicate that one has no sensitive feelings for humanity? Exactly how is this kind of life primitive when affluent white hunters pay thousands of dollars every fall merely for the chance to roam the wilderness shooting at one another in the hopes of also bringing down a deer?

In 1967 I served on the Board of Inquiry for Hunger and Malnutrition in the United States. We discovered that a substantial number of Americans of all colors and backgrounds went to bed hungry every night. Many were living on less than starvation diets and were so weakened that the slightest sickness would carry them off. The black children in the Mississippi delta lands were eating red clay every other day to fill their stomachs to prevent hunger pains. Yet the Agricultural Department had millions of tons of food in giant storehouses that went undistributed every year. Is this type of society more savage than living simply as hunters and fishermen? Is it worth being civilized to have millions of people languishing every year for lack of food while the warehouses are filled with food that cannot be distributed?

Last Christmas in California a federal judge, disgusted at the snarls of red tape that prevented distribution of food to hungry people, ordered a warehouse opened and the food distributed in spite of the pleas of bureaucrats that it was against regulations. In the field of hunger alone the government had better act before hungry people take the law into their own hands.

For years Indian people have sat and listened to speeches by non-Indians that gave glowing accounts of how good the country is now that it is developed. We have listened to people piously tell us that we must drop everything Indian as it is impossible for Indians to maintain their life style in a modern civilized world. We have watched as land was stolen so that giant dams and factories could be built. Every time we have objected to the use of land as a commodity, we have been told that progress is necessary to the American way of life.

Now the laugh is ours. After four centuries of gleeful rape, the white man stands a mere generation away from extinguishing life on this planet. Granted that Indians will also be destroyed—it is not because we did not realize what was happening. It is not because we did not fight back. And it is not because we refused to speak. We have carried our responsibilities well. If people do not choose to listen and instead overwhelm us, then they must bear the ultimate responsibility.

What is the ultimate irony is that the white man must drop his dollar-chasing civilization and return to a simple, tribal, game-hunting, berry-picking life if he is to survive. He must quickly adopt not just the contemporary Indian world view but the ancient Indian world view to survive. He must give up the concept of the earth as a divisible land area that he can market. The lands of the United States must be returned to public ownership and turned into wilderness if man is to live. It will soon be apparent that one man cannot fence off certain areas and do with the land what he will. Such activity will be considered too dangerous to society. Small animals and plants will soon have an equal and perhaps a greater value for human life than humans themselves.

Such a program is, of course, impossible under the American economic and political system at the present time. It would interfere with vested economic interests whose motto has always been "the public be damned." Government policy will continue to advocate cultural oppression against Indian tribes, thinking that the white way of life is best. This past year, five powerful government agencies fought the tiny Lummi tribe of western Washington to prevent it from developing a bay that the tribe owned as a sealife sanctuary. The agencies wanted to build massive projects for commercial use on the bay, the Indians wanted it developed as a conservation area restoring its original food-producing species such as fish, clams, and oysters. Fortunately, the tribe won the fight, much to the chagrin of the Army Corps of Engineers, which makes a specialty of destroying Indian lands.

The white man's conception of nature can be characterized as obscene, but that does not even begin to describe it. It is totally artificial and the very existence of the Astrodome with its artificial grass symbolizes better than words the world visualized by the non-Indian. In any world there is an aspect of violence that cannot be avoided; Nature is arbitrary and men must adjust to her whims. The white man has tried to make Nature adjust to his whims by creating the artificial world of the city. But even here he has failed. Politicians now speak reverently of corridors of safety in the urban areas. They are main lines of transportation where your chance of being robbed or mugged are greatly reduced. Everywhere else there is indiscriminate violence. Urban man has produced even an artificial jungle, where only the fittest or luckiest survive.

With the rising crime rate, even these corridors of safety will disappear. People will only be able to go about in the urban areas in gangs, tribes if you will. Yet the whole situation will be artificial from start to finish. The ultimate conclusion of American society will be that even with respect to personal safety it was much safer and more humane when Indians controlled the whole continent. The only answer will be to adopt Indian ways to survive. For the white man even to exist, he must adopt a total Indian way of life. That is really what he had to do when he came to this land. It is what he will have to do before he leaves it once again.

12 * THE FORMAN MANIFESTO

In 1966, the civil rights movement ground to a halt, subverted by the rising expectations of younger blacks for power developed in their own communities and used on their behalf. After three years of violence and confrontation by the power movements, the situation appeared no better than it had during the civil rights days. Black communities had less power and influence than they did in integration times. Other minority groups were languishing in apathy or being run from pillar to post by sympathetic whites eager to gain a knowledge and therefore entrance into their communities. It was clearly a time for action.

In April, 1969, at a meeting in Detroit aptly named the Black Economic Development Conference, James Forman took the floor and calmly introduced his famous Black Manifesto. Veiled in traditional Marxist terminology, it called for the white churches and synagogues to pay the sum of $500 million to the black community as reparations for the suffering blacks had borne over the past centuries. In May, shortly after the Detroit conference, Forman began his round of the churches, disrupting services and posting notices informing the Christian and Jewish religious leaders that their day of judgment had come.

In the religious headquarters of America everyone was waiting in wild anticipation. Fat little bishops and clergymen who had hitherto been relegated to the ranks of forgotten bureaucrats giggled and twittered with expectation. Righteous veterans of civil rights marches, their lips drawn tight across their faces at the thought of prophecies now come true, stamped around offices collecting their I-told-you-so debts from superiors who had refused to listen to them in the past. Doormen watched the streets anxiously as minutes ticked away. Effeminate liberals could hardly bear the suspense at the thought that HE was coming to confront THEM. The thought of being intellectually ravaged by HIM was too delicious to be borne in solitude. It was a rare cathartic event for which the religious leaders of America had long prayed. They were going to be symbolically crucified!

The aftermath of Forman's visits was predictable. The National Committee of Black Churchmen, an independent body of six hundred black clergymen, supported the manifesto in principle. The ad hoc Black Caucus endorsed it and called for reparations from the black churches as well. The Metropolitan Boston Committee of Black Churchmen called it "perhaps the final opportunity" for churches and synagogues to change the economic order. The World Council of Churches consultation on racism recommended that the central committee of the council endorse the principle of reparations and urged a serious response on the part of American church bodies. The National Council of Churches organized a special committee of sixteen people to study it.

Finally, the clearer heads devised a logical path of escape. An editorial in the *Christian Century* stated that "white Christians are troubled by the manifesto precisely because the love and law of Jesus Christ stamp us as guilty as charged. Further deep down we know that to attempt to pay up could spell the death of the corrupt American church. In such an event the Church might by a miracle of grace be raised anew; *but we can no longer trust in miracles,* sold out as we are to secularism, and we fear for the very survival of our religiously useful institutions. [Emphasis added.]"

The content of the Black Manifesto was for $500 million to be raised by the white churches to be spent by black people as follows:

> $200 million for a Southern land bank to help blacks buy land for agricultural cooperatives in the South.
>
> $130 million to establish a black university in the South.
>
> $40 million for the establishment in Detroit, Atlanta, Los Angeles, and New York of four audiovisual networks.
>
> $40 million for a research skills center and a training center for teaching community organization, photography, movie-making, and other communication skills.
>
> $20 million for a national black labor strike defense fund.
>
> $10 million for the National Welfare Rights Organization.

Later Forman included demands on specific churches to give lands they held to Mexicans and blacks, asking the American Baptist Convention to turn over its land holdings in the South to his organization and demanding that the General Assembly of the United Presbyterian Church give its land in the Southwest to Mexicans and its Southern land to blacks.

Over the summer and fall, church after church was called upon to face the question of reparations. Many churchmen were angry at Forman because they had supported the civil rights movement in previous years under the mistaken belief that passage of certain legislation would solve America's racial problems. Others felt that the churches had not done enough to correct the injustice in American life and that the Black Manifesto was correct in attaching some of the blame for present conditions on them. Most churches split down the middle with laity against reparations and clergy for them.

Forman had hit the key nerve in American society. For years churches had gathered wealth and invested funds in industries and business, claiming that proper stewardship of resources entitled them to adequate income from their funds. Thus churches had become major owners of wealth and some investments were diametrically opposed to stands that certain churches had taken. Some churches, for example, that frowned on alcohol, had investments in breweries and distilleries. Others that opposed slum housing owned extensive tracts of real estate in large cities.

Over the last decade, theologians proclaimed that God was dead. Some spoke of the end of the Christian Era and others called it the end of the Protestant Era. Secular religion had triumphed over traditional religion and everyone recognized that fact. Yet it took James Forman to shake the churches alive, and when he did, they suddenly found that they had much more to lose by admitting their demise than they could gain by avoiding the question entirely.

The result of the Black Manifesto was a series of pious declarations that while the churches totally rejected the Black Economic Development Conference, they would see that it received funds by setting up stalking-horse organizations to funnel funds through. This device made it appear that they were not really supporting the demands made by Forman. Thus bishops and clergy could in "good faith" tell their parishioners that they had rejected the idea of reparations while frantically shoveling the funds out the back door.

This type of deception pinpointed the problem of contemporary society. The noble administrators of the American religious establishment could not face themselves. A straightforward alliance with Forman was impossible because the churches were captives of the disintegrating American culture. For centuries they had carefully hedged their bets, appearing at one time for human rights and other times as the ally of secular forces of oppression. The pity is that they did not do this maliciously, for they did not know the difference. Forman, unfortunately, did.

American Christianity has been the captive of the State since the inception of the Republic. The first colonies were dominated by certain religious bodies. When the new Republic was formed, many maintained their stranglehold over the voting franchise for decades. Even today the Governor of Maryland is the legal head of the Episcopal Church in that state. The desire for religious freedom that initially drove the colonists across the seas was transformed into political individualism in the Constitution, so that the two ideas, political and religious freedom of the individual, became welded together from the very beginning. Ideologically it was impossible that the churches could judge the actions of the government or that the government would become hostile to the churches. Theology and political ideology were identical. If one fell, the other was sure to go.

Churches have long received a tax-exempt status as part of their recognition from the particular state. Originally, this exemption was justified, because churches in large measure provided for education where the state was unable or unwilling to provide it. When the public schools were instituted, the tax exemption simply continued, so that the church and state simply split a certain percentage of income each year by means of the taxing powers, the church receiving contributions which are deductible from annual income.

This alliance has become so important that the state has usually come immediately to the rescue whenever the churches have been in danger. In recent years there have been attacks on the tax exemption of religious bodies, and government has rushed in to assist the churches. A recent case involving the challenge of church exemption from real estate taxes saw attorney-generals of thirty-seven states leap into action with supporting briefs proclaiming the benefits of church exemptions to society at large.

While we have talked about the separation of church and state, we have not in fact had such a separation. Religion has shifted to take in every change of the winds, so that its obedience to American culture and political trends is apparent. As life styles have changed, so has the theology of the churches. Manifest destiny became social gospel with barely a backward glance. At the start of the civil rights movement, while Eisenhower was still President, the churches waited out the storm. When Kennedy and Johnson were in office, churches were active because the Presidents were active in civil rights.

In the last decade, churches have leaned over backward to pay homage to the revolt of young people. Clergy had to be "hip." Nuns and priests came out of hiding, dropped long-standing habits, and appeared in slacks and skirts. Where they had played baseball in their religious uniforms in the 1950s, they now became civil rights marchers and pickets. The foremost characteristic of the churches over the last decade was their discovery that they had to be relevant and follow every development with understanding and involvement. The most popular theologian of the last decade, Malcom Boyd, performed his ministry at nightclubs and bars, and followed the trend to the very end, finally inquiring whether God was running with him.

In attempting to comprehend the changes in American life, religious leaders have made use of every device of modern living to ensure that religion keeps abreast of cultural developments. Churches have set up data banks, given out green stamps, advocated black theology, sought federal support for their schools, and installed jukeboxes in their churches to assure contemporary society that they really cared. During the heyday of the civil rights movement, the folk mass was introduced into the churches and guitars twanged meaningfully with rock songs that made Jesus the hit of the movement. Recently, in the style of paperbacks, the Gospel has been put out as *Thoughts from Chairman Jesus.*

Theologians learning that young people are advocating a revolution counsel a theology of revolution. Even symbols of traditional Christian faith have become transformed to suit the demands of activist groups in society, and Father Groppi, militant priest of Milwaukee, has advocated the creation of a black Christ to fit the needs of the black community. A picture exhibited by the Defense Department entitled "The Next Supper" shows Jesus smoking pot surrounded by Spider Man, Charlie Brown, Bugs Bunny, Jughead, Archie, Captain Midnight, Mickey Mouse, Superman, Santa Claus, Thor, Scrooge McDuck, and Batman.

The surrender of symbolism marks the complete collapse of the Christian religion to the forces of the secular world. It is now impossible to discern where the world ends and religion begins. Churches have become political forces in the modern world and political forces have become religious. The Republican Convention of 1968 was characterized by an ending prayer by Billy Graham followed by a swing version of "Glory, Glory, Hallelujah," so that the transition from religion to politics and back went virtually unnoticed by television viewers.

With this development has come the corresponding movement of people from organized religion to astrology, numerology, reincarnation, palm-reading, I Ching, Tarot cards, witchcraft, and drugs, in an effort to realize in some manner a reality and guidance beyond the self. T-groupism, Karma, nirvana, occultism, the Upanishads, peyote, yoga, Zen, the cabala, and reality therapy have become household words.

The result of this confusion is that we have largely neglected facts that continue to stare us in the face. In searching for a religion in society, we have become captured by the tangible things of life, so that questions primarily religious no longer appear to be so. With American Christianity and the American government largely welded together in a holy alliance, a threat against one would appear to be a threat against the other. Thus any disrupting force that appeared to have the capability of changing one side of the equation would appear to be a threat against the delicate balance that has been achieved.

No movement in this century has been so unsettling as has the civil rights movement. Demanding equality of opportunity, the black community struggled to gain its rights in terms of integration and separatism. It has been thwarted in both directions. Integration was based upon the Christian doctrine of the brotherhood of man. Separatism was based upon the Muslim doctrine of man. Thus the two basic alternatives stemming from the corruption of Jewish religion have been instrumental in defining the alternatives of development of the black community in the political arena.

Symbolizing the movements have been two outstanding leaders, Martin Luther King, Jr., and Malcolm X. They are the two major black leaders who have been assassinated. During the years when H. Rap Brown habitually carried shotguns on airplanes, when Stokely Carmichael threatened trouble, when the Panthers had shoot-outs with police, few of these people were killed or even shot at. Yet the two black leaders who most represented religious ideologies were carefully assassinated to prevent them from carrying out their tasks. It would appear that the thing that American society most fears is the rise of a religious figure who will rip the veil from people's eyes and make them face the truth about themselves. Thus when Timothy Leary formed the League for Spiritual Discovery . . .

The real issue to be faced today is thus a religious issue. Backlash against the power movements is not as much against specific minority groups as it is against the desire of minority groups to withdraw into their own communities and discover a way of life all their own—one which might prove superior to the traditional American way of life. Every time a member of a minority group demands a status for his group, he calls down upon himself the disbelief and anger of white America, because he is talking about his group achieving something that America has yet to achieve.

The frantic persecution of youth for taking drugs and smoking pot is not for the protection of society, since alcohol does much more damage than does pot and drugs. Rather the frantic chase of the older generation is to keep young people from tearing off the ceremonial masks that hide a religionless people from themselves. Demanding peace in Vietnam has brought the police screaming into the night in vast armies ready to destroy dissenters because they dare to reveal that the nation has no soul. It is not simply a disagreement over foreign policy.

Now the older generation is carefully nudging young people to consider the problem of pollution instead of the Vietnam War as the next "big issue," as if young people can be pushed from fad to fad without realizing what they are doing. Yet even in this area the call of the land brings a religious understanding that surpasses everything ever advocated by the religious-political combine that has directed this nation over its lifetime. Young people may mushroom the pollution issue completely out of hand because they may come to understand the necessity of religious people to be intimately related to their lands.

The deaths of Martin Luther King, Jr., and Malcolm X indicate better than any other sign that the crisis in American society is deeper than racism or violence. They indicate the beginning of a new world religion on this continent that will create its own mythology and symbolism and sweep the world with its vision. Such a religion would be diametrically opposed to everything that American society has affirmed. Hence it was necessary for some forces in society to destroy the religious leaders in the black community who could have conceivably triggered that religion. In the same manner the semireligious awe in which the Kennedys moved caused people to reevaluate their position in regard to American society, and worked directly toward their destruction.

We are trapped between ages of religious mythology. We live in a time when old nations are breaking up and new nations are being formed. It thus becomes imperative to destroy anyone who appears to be developing a sense of life values that does not coincide with what we have come to regard as our own. Martin Luther King, Jr., discerned this change and in his last book noted that "if the society changes its concepts by placing responsibility on its system, not on the individual, and guarantees secure employment or a minimum income, dignity will come within reach of all."

Dignity of the individual was supposed to be guaranteed by both the Christian religion and the American Constitution. The fact that it could not be universally realized by all men has led to the search for a life style that can produce this result. Hence the changes that we see in American society have very deep channels that cover up the movement toward a new world order. Whether this is comprehended by the ideology of the Third World movement is difficult to say. The fact that such a movement is happening on this continent rather than any other indicates that it will be influenced by the land and people among whom it arises.

The pattern of relationships between minority groups and

white society has often run according to the Moses myth. Members of minority groups have been sent to school with the idea that they would eventually create black, Indian, or Mexican Moseses who would lead their people to the promised land of the white man. But it has not worked out that way. Moses left Egypt in ruins, and wherever the new religious leader wanders he will also leave this nation in ruins.

For that reason it is very dangerous to be alive today. That a new religion is rising is certain. Where it will arise and who will be its prophet is undetermined. For its own protection American society must watch day and night for any sign of radical change that might indicate its demise. This is the real nerve which James Forman hit in his concept of reparations. Reparations is indeed the last chance that religious America has to save itself. By buying off minority groups it can lull the people back to sleep and buy time.

Social change from individualism into a modern form of tribalism or feudalism contains within itself the seeds of destruction and salvation. With modern electronic media there is no chance for us to turn back, since we are being tribalized by our very existence in the modern world. It is only as we rush through this period of change with a minimum of conflict that we will be able to make the transitional jump from one world system to another. Otherwise we shall surely perish.

The crucial thing to note is that we have passed the point of no return, so that we cannot go home again. Every effort that is made to adjust society to familiar patterns only increases the speed with which change occurs. A repressive government may very well invoke the conditions we are trying to avoid. Certainly repression of drugs has only resulted in the increased use of drugs. Repression of sex has created a generation of sexual athletes. Repression of alcohol created the Roaring Twenties. Instead of repression and conformity we should open as many options as possible to as many groups and interests as possible. By creating the most flexible situation we can, we may find the tools and techniques to survive the changes ahead.

APPENDIX

THE MOVEMENT in American society often appears to be shifting toward one pole while it is in fact moving steadily toward the opposite conclusion. It would have appeared ridiculous to have written on the implications of the "Power" movements some four years after they had been headline news had there not been something inherently different in the ideology of power with the minority group communities that American society had not yet understood.

While newspaper headlines often wear ideas out long before they would ordinarily perish, it is significant that in the more thoughtful segments of our society the philosophical base upon which Carmichael and Hamilton placed their new theory of race relations has continually expanded. Thus it was no surprise when a federal district court in Texas came down with a landmark decision in the case of *Cisneros* v. *Corpus Christi Independent School District* to the effect that the Mexican-American community, which had previously been disguised as "white" in the statistics which in our society tend to identify groups and problems, was an identifiable group with specific rights inherent in itself.

The ruling should not have been a landmark. A century ago, at the conclusion of the Mexican War, there should have been an effort by the United States to give special effect to the Treaty of Guadalupe Hidalgo so that the rights that Mexican citizens had had under the Mexican regime could have been upheld under American citizenship. In that way immigrant Mexicans could have settled in the Mexican towns in New Mexico, Texas, Arizona, and California with their rights as members of a particular city-state defined.

In a number of treaties and statutes the rights of Mexican-Americans have been clearly marked out. In particular, the Osage Treaty of 1808 specifically recognized the titles of citizens of Spain even above the Indian title of occupancy. But history, as we have seen, has not allowed the larger minority communities to receive the guarantees of the Constitution which have been made available to whites. Thus the conflict, now joined, will probably continue. The minority groups will continue to explore the implications of group rights under the present interpretation of the Constitution. With the present administration intent on rolling back half a century of integrationist legal philosophy and attempting to pack the court with calculated mediocrities whose sole merit to appointment is their desire to return to the thrilling plantation days of yesteryear, it would appear that the separatist elements in the minority groups now have several decades to create a thoroughgoing ideology of the rights of groups.

In view of the impending disaster in ecology, this development of group rights may prove to be the salvation of the survivors of modern technological society. If hostile elements are faced by a group, then integrity, customs, and semisovereignty can be built into smaller groups of people so that upon the final irrational dissolution of American society these people will survive. Whether the economic distribution system will be so thoroughly destroyed as to reduce modern society to absolute tribalism, or whether a fragment of that system will exist leaving us with a modified feudalism, is the question that we now face.

With the young singing such religiously oriented songs as "Spirit in the Sky," "Bridge over Troubled Waters," and "Let It Be," and the added emphasis on Woodstock nationality, one could expect the next landmark case to be involved with the rights of young people freely to act on deeply held moral convictions: and witness the Supreme Court decision on June 15, 1970, upholding the right to conscientious objection on ethical as well as religious grounds. An additional thrust might be made from within one of the minority groups toward legal support of cultural values that radically differ from accepted WASP values. Already the movement toward reform of abortion laws has broken through and produced a flood of legislation that radically reorients traditional values of sex, marriage, and life itself.

I have included the recent decision with regard to the Mexican-American community in this appendix to show that the basic ideology that has been presented in this book is not only vitally alive but will continue to exert significant influence on modern social thinking. There will be new tribes and new turf—in our lifetime.

CISNEROS v. CORPUS CHRISTI INDEPENDENT SCHOOL DISTRICT
June 5, 1970

In civil action No. 68-C-95, a civil rights class action, the following will constitute the findings of fact and conclusions of law, and may be amended and/or supplemented at a later date, but these findings today will control and determine the disposition of the issues before us.

Firstly, this court finds that it has jurisdiction and that this is a proper case action under Rule 23 of the Federal Rules of Civil Procedure.

Needless to say, this court considers this to be a most important case. Not only because of the great interest that has been manifested by the large attendance of citizens in the courtroom, and the amount of time and space the news media have devoted to the coverage of the trial, but the court realizes and understands that we are considering two of the most important aspects and interests of the school patrons and also the school administration: the taxes of money and the children.

Because it is an important case I want again to express my appreciation for the effort of the attorneys who have appeared here, not only for their cooperation in providing the court with all the relevant and pertinent evidence, voluminous data and statistics, but also for well-written briefs and the expeditious manner in which the evidence was presented.

This type of legal controversy, which is prevalent all over the country, has finally come to the City of Corpus Christi, as it has come to many other communities over our land, and the magnitude of the problem is reflected in the great volume of litigation and opinions which we lawyers are familiar with.

Because the United States District Courts are under a mandate to expedite this type of litigation, and because this court knows that school has just closed and the summer semester is beginning, and that the 1970–71 school year term will begin in three months, the court believes it will serve the ends of justice, as well as the interest of the parties to this lawsuit, especially the school administration, to present this opinion orally and not to wait to have it typed, reproduced, and printed.

Although, as you could realize, it has not been an easy task. I have had the advantage of three weeks of night-and-day studying of these exhibits, this voluminous data, taking two briefcases to Miami, constantly reading the opinions and having them available to me as they are published. And also, thanks to the attorneys in the case, of having the advantage of having daily copy made of the proceedings and testimony.

One great advantage and help to the court was the way and manner all the statistical evidence was worked and cataloged at the beginning of the trial, and which was offered and stipulated to early in the trial, and which was available to the court for study for these three weeks.

We also were fortunate in having available every recent appellate decision concerning these matters.

In reaching the decision in this case, I have carefully weighed and considered all of the evidence, and each and every witness's testimony was considered in the light of common sense, the witness's experience and qualifications, his interest in the case, his demeanor on the witness stand, whether or not he answered the questions directly and unequivocally, or whether he was vague or evasive, or whether he equivocated, and whether or not it appeared accurately in comparison with statistical data and evidence that was not disputed.

Although the statistical data and evidence was largely undisputed, I find as a matter of fact for the record that the data presented by the plaintiff is accurate and correct as to student populations, percentage of ethnic groups, that is, as we have called them in this trial, Anglo, Negro, and Mexican-American, locations of schools, and the makeup of the student population, the population, the location and ethnic patterns of general population within this area, the number of teachers, the schools they are assigned to, and the ethnic background of each teacher in each school, and the location of past and present boundaries, the time and cost of construction of new schools, the cost of renovating of old schools, the number of children bused in the past and in the present, and who they were and who they are.

I especially find the plaintiff's exhibits No. 4, 4-A, 4-C, and 4-D as accurate and very illuminating.

The same is true for plaintiff's exhibits 6-A, 6-B, 6-C, and plaintiff's exhibit 7, also plaintiff's exhibit No. 35, and plaintiff's exhibit 36.

The court accepts as true and correct the other objective data and statistics offered by the plaintiff.

Of course, most of this evidence, if not all, was furnished by the defendant, and the court is deeply appreciative of the cooperation, of the long, tiresome work that the school administration had to undertake to furnish this data.

I also find that the defendant's objective statistical evidence is true and correct, such as defendant's exhibits 1, 2, 2-A, 3, 3-A, 4, 5, 6, 7, 8, 9, 10, 11, 14, 15 and 16.

The plaintiff's and defendant's exhibits as mentioned mainly include objective evidentiary data over which there is no dispute, as I understand the parties, but I do understand that each side contends there are different factual and legal implications and conclusions to be drawn from this objective statistical evidence which the court, of course, will have to decide.

As to the other exhibits, the court will consider them and give to them whatever weight and credibility, as well as relevancy, the court feels they deserve in deciding the factual and legal issues involved.

Finally, the court recognizes that experts similarly trained, similarly educated, and with good intentions, do disagree over fundamental issues. And that is not only true in the field of education, but this court sees it every day when we have trials with experts, where they disagree over the most basic and fundamental issues. And there has been some disagreement manifested during this trial that just could not be reconciled, and the court must use its own judgment to see that justice is done after carefully considering all of the evidence.

Although there has been somewhat of a lack of basic empirical evidence which has been validated or demonstrated by experience or results, and the educators spoke of that often during the trial, the court must decide this case on the evidence before it.

Now to the issues in the case. It appears to the court that the controlling and ultimate issues, stated in general terms, are as follows:

Firstly, can Brown, 347 U.S. 483,* and its progeny apply to Mexican-Americans in the Corpus Christi Independent School District, or stated in another way, is Brown limited to Negroes only?

Secondly, if Brown can apply to Mexican-Americans, does it, under the facts of this case?

In another way, assuming Brown applies to Mexican-Americans, are the Mexican-American students segregated or in a dual school system?

Thirdly, because I think most of us agree that the Negroes in Corpus Christi are protected by the Fourteenth Amendment to the Constitution under Brown, as was a case involving blacks and whites, and later the Supreme Court and Fifth Circuit cases, the question or issue here is, do we have a dual or unitary school system as it affects Negroes in Corpus Christi?

Further, or fourthly, if we do have a dual school system here as defined by recent Fifth Circuit cases, and that Negroes and Mexican-Americans are denied their constitutional rights under the Fourteenth Amendment, is this a *de jure* or *de facto* dual or segregated school system?

And finally, if we do have a dual system, how can the court, and under what plans and programs, disestablish a dual school system and establish and maintain a unitary school system in contemplation and compliance with the recent Supreme Court and Fifth Circuit opinions?

And so, in determining the first general issue in this case, which is whether Brown can apply to Mexican-Americans in the Corpus Christi Independent School District, the court now makes the

* Brown *v.* Board of Education, decided by the United States Supreme Court on May 17, 1954, overturned the doctrine of "separate but equal."

following observations concerning the implication of Brown to this issue.

This court reads Brown to mean that when a state undertakes to provide public school education, this education must be made available to all students on equal terms, and that segregation of any group of children in such public schools on the basis of their being of a particular race, cult, national origin, or of some readily identifiable ethnic minority group, or class, deprives these children of the guarantees of the Fourteenth Amendment as set out in Brown, and subsequent decisions, even though the physical facilities and other tangible factors may be equal.

Although these cases speak in terms of race and color, we must remember that these cases were only concerned with blacks and whites, but it is clear to this court that these cases are not limited to race and color alone.

In this case, if the proof shows that the Mexican-Americans in the Corpus Christi Independent School District are an identifiable ethnic minority group, and for this reason have been segregated and discriminated against in the schools, in the manner that Brown prohibits, then they are certainly entitled to all the protection announced in Brown. Thus, Brown can apply to Mexican-American students in public schools.

Having decided that Brown can apply to Mexican-American students in public schools, the court now must determine whether under the facts of this case the Mexican-American students in the Corpus Christi Independent School District do fall within the protection of Brown.

The court finds from the evidence that these Mexican-American students are an identifiable ethnic minority class sufficient to bring them within the protection of Brown.

It is clear to this court that Mexican-Americans, or Americans with Spanish surnames, or whatever they are called, or whatever they would like to be called, Latin Americans, or several other new names of identification, and, parenthetically, the court will take notice that this naming for identification phenomena is similiar to that experienced in the Negro groups, black, Negro, colored, and now black again, with an occasional insulting epithet that is used less and less by white people in the South, fortunately. Occasionally you hear the word "Mex" still spoken in a derogatory way in the Southwest.

It is clear to this court that these people for whom we have used the word Mexican-Americans to describe their class, group, or segment of our population, are an identifiable ethnic minority in the United States, and especially so in the Southwest and in Texas and in Corpus Christi. This is not surprising; we can notice and identify their physical characteristics, their language, their predominant religion, their distinct culture, and, of course, their Spanish surnames. And if there were any doubt in this court's mind, this court could take notice, which it does, of the congressional enactments, governmental studies and commissions on this problem. And also the opinions, such as Hernandez v. Texas, 347 U.S. 475, a 1954 case; Judge Allred's decision in this case, Hernandez v. Driscoll Consolidated Independent School District, Civil Action No. 13840; unpublished, Keys *et al.* v. School District No. 1, Civil Action 1449, District of Colorado; Westminster School of Orange County v. Mendez, 161 Federal 2nd 774, Ninth Circuit, 1947; and also, and very importantly, the recent federal government's intervention in Marcos Perez *et al.* v. Sonora Independent School District No. 6, 224 Civil, San Angelo Division of the Northern District of Texas.

This court further finds that the Mexican-American students in the Corpus Christi Independent School District are now separated and segregated to a degree prohibited by the Fourteenth Amendment in all three levels of the school system, elementary, junior high, and senior high. It is obvious to the court from the evidence that the Mexican-Americans have been historically discriminated against as a class in the Southwest and in Texas, and in the Corpus Christi district. This court is convinced that this history of discrimination as given by Dr. Thomas Carter, Dr. Hector Garcia, and Mr. Paul Montemayor is substantially correct.

Not only do I find that Mexican-Americans have been discriminated against as a class, I further find that because they are an identifiable ethnic minority that they are more susceptible to discrimination and this is not common to Mexican-Americans and Negroes alone, but it appears from history that any identifiable minority group, that is a different person, whether it be of racial, ethnic, religious, or national origin, may quite often suffer from this problem.

It seems to this court that the Mexican-American organizations, such as the LULACs and the G.I. Forum, and now MAYO, were called into being in response to this problem. This is why, perhaps, we are having so many studies, so many hearings, so many government commissions studying these problems, and so many publications and books being published concerning this very real problem.

Fortunately, the objective manifestation of this type of discrimination is gradually disappearing from our society. Nevertheless, this historical pattern of discrimination has contributed to the present substantial segregation of Mexican-Americans in our schools. This segregation has resulted in a dual school system.

The court also finds that the Negro students in the Corpus Christi Independent School District are also segregated to a degree prohibited by law, which causes this to be a dual rather than a unitary school system.

The court's finding that the Mexican-American and Negro students are substantially segregated from the remaining student population of this district is based primarily upon the undisputed statistical evidence. This is also, and I also find, true of the faculty.

The court is of the opinion that placing Negroes and Mexican-Americans in the same school does not achieve a unitary system. As contemplated by law, a unitary school district can be achieved here only by substantial integration of the Negroes and Mexican-Americans with the remaining student population of the district.

As to whether or not the segregation which has resulted in this dual system is *de facto* or *de jure*, the court is of the opinion that some of the segregation was of a *de facto* nature; that is, because of the socioeconomic factors which caused Negroes and Mexican-Americans to live in the corridor, which we have described here as where they live, and similar to the ghettos of other cities, and of the pattern of the geographical and demographic expansion of the city towards the south and southwest.

But this segregated and dual school district has its real roots in the minds of men, that is, in the failure of the school system to anticipate and correct the imbalancing that was developing. The court is of the firm opinion that administrative decisions by the school board in drawing boundaries, locating new schools, building new schools, and renovating old schools in the predominantly Negro and Mexican-American part of town; in providing an elastic and flexible subjective transfer system that resulted in some Anglo children being allowed to avoid the ghetto, or corridor, schools by busing some students, by providing one or more optional transfer zones which resulted in Anglos being able to avoid Negro [and] Mexican-American schools and not allowing Mexican-Americans or Negroes the option of spending extraordinarily large sums of money, which resulted in intensifying and perpetuating a segregated dual school system; by assigning Negro and Mexican-American teachers in disparity ratios to these segregated schools; and the further failure to employ a sufficient number of Negro and Mexican-American schoolteachers; and the failure to provide a majority-to-minority transfer rule; all of which, regardless of all explanations and regardless of all expressions of good intentions, was calculated, and did maintain and promote a dual school system.

Therefore this court finds as a matter of fact and law that the Corpus Christi Independent School District is a *de jure* segregated school system.

The defendants have attempted to show that the Negroes and Mexican-Americans are spread throughout the city. To what [ever] extent this is true, nevertheless the undisputed statistics show that the Negroes and Mexican-Americans are substantially segregated in the school system. So this would mean that the schoolhouse is more segregated than the neighborhoods.

The defendants argued that they did not have the benefit of hindsight, which we all appreciate, but this court feels that there were sufficient warnings given to the school board by interested citizens and groups to alert them to this problem, which any school board member or superintendent should know might be a problem in this day and age.

This court is not here to place blame, criticize, or find fault, but this suit was brought to this court by the plaintiff's alleging a denial of rights protected by the Fourteenth Amendment. And it is this court's duty to adjudicate these grievances. The courts do not go out and look for these controversial problems to solve, they are brought to the courthouse by human beings with a grievance, and that is where they should be brought.

This court knows that board members change from time to time; this court knows that in our complex society of today, of large institutions, that we do have problems of personal responsibility or of collective responsibility, individual fault or corporate fault, private blame or institutional blame. Moral man and a moral society, as [Reinhold] Niebuhr puts it, is still with us. But whatever was the personal and individual intentions of the school board members, who I noted did not testify in this case, the board had the ultimate responsibility, and I find that the board of trustees of the Corpus Christi Independent School District has not discharged its heavy burden to explain its preferences for what this court finds is a segregated and dual school system.

I cannot and do not accept the explanations given by the school administration for not only maintaining a segregated school system and dual school system, but really what appears to me to be a program which will intensify and magnify the problem as time goes on.

This court is of the opinion that there are reasonable available methods to effect a unitary system, and this court finds that this dual system can be disestablished without significant administrative, educational, economic, or transportation costs. And I appreciated the plaintiff's bringing the court's attention to the fact that they are not here asking for a large number of children to be bused, and neither is the court, and it is obvious that the faculty and the administrative staff is even more segregated than the schools. There is no real dispute here.

The school must assign Negro and Mexican-American teachers

throughout the system on the same ratio of percentages they are in the total teacher and staff population. Furthermore, the school board must immediately take steps to employ more Negro and Mexican-American teachers.

And as to the dire effects the defendant claims will result if there is more transportation of students than is presently done, the court says that the children who are being bused now make no such claims, nor have I been shown any harmful effects on the individual children that will outweigh the harmful effects on the Negro and Mexican-American child who is in a segregated and dual system. That is my opinion after giving careful attention to all of the testimony of the experts.

The physical and social inconveniences that some children might suffer will not be as severe or as prolonged as compared to the psychological and emotional trauma, and scarring and crippling, that minority children suffer when they feel they are rejected or not accepted.

As to the educational benefits: this court is of the opinion that the Anglo child and the Negro and the Mexican-American child will benefit by a unitary system, and I think the plaintiff's statistics and study show this, especially those on the amount of schooling Anglos and Mexican-Americans get in duration of time. Our nation is becoming polarized and fragmented, and this has the effect of radicalizing many of our young people. It is not enough today to pay lip service to the Constitution by tokenism.

While many of our institutions have a tendency to divide us—religious institutions, social institutions, economic institutions, political institutions—the public school institutions, as I see it, is the one unique institution which has the capacity to unite this nation and to unite this diverse and pluralistic society that we have. We are not a homogeneous people, we are a heterogeneous people: we have many races, many religions, many colors in America. Here in the public school system as young Americans, they can study, play together, interact, they will get to know one another, to respect the others' differences, to tolerate each other even though [of] a different race, color, religious, social, or ethnic status.

But be that as it may, the Supreme Court has resolved that problem for the district court by saying that separate educational facilities are inherently unequal and therefore unconstitutional.

Therefore the court finds for the plaintiffs and the injunctive relief prayed for will be granted.

Because the courts, especially in the South, are finding that a biracial or human relations committee appointed by the court can aid the school boards and the courts through these trying times, and in these complex problems of creating a unitary system and maintaining it, this court is of the opinion that a human relations committee appointed by this court will be of great help. And, therefore, the plaintiff and defendant will immediately provide the court with a list of fifteen names each of patrons of the Corpus Christi Independent School District, which list shall include the name, address, and telephone number of each person, and each list shall include five Negroes, five Anglos, and five Mexican-Americans, and the court will choose from this list two names from each of the five names submitted which will provide the court with a committee of twelve persons, four of which will be Anglo, four will be Negro, and four will be Mexican-Americans. The court will charge this twelve-member human relations committee with the responsibility of investigating and consulting and advising with the school board periodically with respect to all matters tending to promote and to maintain the operations of a unitary school system, which will satisfy the law.

Because this opinion and partial final judgment involves a controlling question of law, as to which there is substantial grounds for differences of opinion, insofar as this court is of the opinion that Mexican-Americans are an identifiable ethnic class who have suffered *de jure* and *de facto* segregation and who are protected as a class under the Fourteenth Amendment and the laws of the United States, and who are now being subjected to a dual school system in violation of the Fourteenth Amendment and the laws of the United States, and the court, that the court has found that they should be and are protected, and that they should be in a unitary school system, and therefore, the court is of the opinion that the defendant may utilize the procedures of 28

United States Code Annotated, Section 1292, to the end that such an interlocutory immediate appeal, if the defendant should desire to do so, would materially advance the ultimate determination of this court. But this opinion and the judgment to be entered immediately will not be stayed pending this interlocutory appeal, if one is made, because of the defendant's right to an emergency appeal under Rule 2 and Related Rules and Practices of the Court of Appeals for the Fifth Circuit, and further because the parties have already had the transcript made of all the testimony and the voluminous evidentiary data which has been introduced into evidence is already cataloged and in such a manner that time will not be a real problem.

The plaintiff and defendant will submit to this court by July the 15th a final plan which will achieve a unitary school system which will be educationally, administratively, and economically reasonable. It shall include a majority-to-minority transfer rule as suggested in Singleton *et al.* v. Jackson Municipal Separate School District, No. 29226, decided on May the 5th, 1970, by the Court of Appeals for the Fifth Circuit.

The deputy courtroom clerk of the court, Miss Baker, shall select the twelve names which will comprise the human relations committee by arranging all six stacks of five names in an alphabetical manner and taking the top two names from each stack which will provide a human relations committee of twelve persons, four of which will be Negro, four will be Anglo, and four will be Mexican. The clerk will communicate immediately with these twelve persons and inform them that the court wishes that they serve on this human relations committee, and if any should decline to serve, the court then will take the next name from the particular stack. The court has not seen nor looked at those names and does not know who they are, except the court did ask the lawyers, and do ask the lawyers to give us competent people, which I am sure they have done.

The court reporter will immediately transcribe these oral findings of fact and conclusions of law in this opinion and will file it with the clerk of the court and provide each party with a copy.

This court shall retain jurisdiction of this case until it is satisfied that the dual system has been disestablished and a unitary system is in existence for a sufficient length of time to indicate the dual system will not tend to be reestablished.

The plaintiff will submit to the court immediately after consultation with the defendant's attorneys, and after giving the defendant an opportunity to approve it as to form, an appropriate judgment not inconsistent with this opinion.

The court is adjourned.